# 222
# TIPS
# FOR DOING
# BUSINESS
ON THE
# INTERNET

Version 2.0

SEBASTIAN PINCETTI • SILVINA RODRIGUEZ PICARO

# 222
# TIPS
# FOR DOING
# BUSINESS
## ON THE
# INTERNET

## How to master Marketing 2.0

© **222 Tips for doing Business on the Internet**
Version 2.0
Sebastián Pincetti • Silvina Rodriguez Picaro

ISBN: 978-0-9791956-9-3

Design, Layout: SRP Communication & Brand Design
www.srpdesign.com

Images: Shutterstock, Istockphoto and SRP Communication & Brand Design
Charts: SRP Interactive

York House Press
1266 E. Main St. 700R
Stamford, CT 06902

# DEDICATION

**To our customers**

who place their trust in us day in day out, affording
us the chance to grow with them. They are the main
reason why we continue to learn, staying up to speed
in an ever changing world.


**For Kayla**

"

"Success is not the key to happiness.
Happiness is the key to success.
If you love what you are doing,
you will be successful."

**Albert Schweitzer**

# TABLE OF CONTENTS

"

"What's dangerous
is not to evolve."

**Jeff Bezos**
CEO of Amazon.com

# FOREWORD I

By **Claudia Gioia-Wencelblat**

Managing Director, Burson-Marsteller Miami

**222 Tips for doing Business on the Internet** reminds me of the classic Woody Allen film: "Every Thing You Always Wanted to Know About Sex But Were Afraid to Ask". In the case of online communication—such as when we put together a Website—we're not only faced with the challenge of overcoming our fear of asking questions, but with not knowing who to ask!

The authors help us to unveil what we need to know in a simple and practical way. The pages that follow seek to answer all the questions we face when developing a Website that's to be effective for the owner as well as for the user! A well-conceived Website in terms of design, use, technical operation and content can be the difference between losing money and making a profit.

This book is meant to be read, consulted, challenged and even re-read, written on and shared. So when you finish your Website following these Tips, you will feel the satisfaction of a job well done. Now take a deep breath.

# FOREWORD II

By **David Moffly**,

CEO of BaebleMusic.com

Working as a publisher on the Web is a lot like playing your favorite board game Checkers in 3–D. On the face of it the Web is this phenomenon that most of us have gotten familiar with and use with varying degrees of comfort every day. I remember 1998 as the Dotcom bubble was reaching its height the obnoxious evangelists went around saying that the Web "changed everything". They were all out of business in three years but the kernel of what they said was more than right. The impact of the Web is ubiquitous on a global scale. Entire businesses, technologies and creative destruction have evolved and sprung out of it seems nowhere. Who could have imagined fifteen years ago that entire multibillion dollar companies would be formed around the simple idea of allowing people to connect to their friends on the Web?

In 1998 with a stock image licensing company I was running at the time we put up our first Website. The process and business objective felt very straight forward at the time. We were a photography licensing business and we were seeking to extend our distribution and storefront from printed catalogs to the Web. The great premise was that we were taking cost out of this business by no longer having to edit, print and ship tens of thousands catalogs around the world to our customers and agents. We viewed the Web as another distribution channel for our images that would allow more of our millions of images in our files to be seen by the professional customers we serviced. The design and implementation of this Website was straight forward and highly labor intensive. This was our first site and I am sure our design agency's as well. Once the basic information design was blocked out by the design firm, we hired a Web company in San Francisco to implement the design and pull the project together. We all learned a lot of new vocabulary along the way and months later we had a new site. What was missing in this discussion were discussions on SEM and SEO strategies. Google had just been founded and AOL was king at the time making millions selling keywords to large consumer facing organizations like Post–AOL Keyword "Wheaties".

Thirteen years have passed and the changes in the Web have been geometric. Google is king and AOL is a marginalized player trying to re-invent itself as a Web savvy media company. We have all be subject for the last several years to the relentless buzz mongering of the media telling us that we are now at Web 2.0 and the techno elite are talking about Web 3.0 built on top of the next generation of super high speed Web currently connecting some Universities around the world. Networking, video, next generation media consumption are what everyone is trying to figure out. Large companies are pouring money into these areas as fast as they can afford to.

This change and growth has left many of us confused and intimidated by the seemingly simple business need of connecting to prospects, messaging, marketing and selling over the Web. The Web has today has its own extremely confusing lexicon that evolves seemingly every day. If you don't live in the world you just have no good guide to the endless and crucial sets of decisions that need to be made as you build a site, create a viral campaign otherwise try and communicate across the Web. SRP Interactive has formulated a common sense approach of tools and tricks for the Web that is worth taking the time to study and become acquainted with as you think through your objectives and strategy for the Web. Simple tools like this can save you valuable time money and frustration as you approach this most vital of mediums.

# THE YIN YANG OF THE INTERNET

As in Yin Yang, things on the Internet are not always black or white, true or false, and realities change all the time; frequently, much more than what we wished for. According to the ancient Chinese, Yin and Yang represents an understanding of how the world works. The external circle represents the whole, and the white and black shapes inside the circle represent the interaction of the two energies, called Yin (represented in black) and Yang (represented in white). Both energies are what make things happen. Nothing is totally white or totally black and Yin and Yang energies cannot exist without one another.

While Yin is dark, passive, cold, contracted, weak and pointing downwards; Yang is bright, active, warm, expansive, strong and points upwards. The shape with which each of these energies is represented with their thinner extremes, gives the sensation of continuous movement, just like in energies in reality, making things flow, turning nights into days, making objects contract and expand themselves or changing temperature. The Yin and Yang represent the nature of things. Nothing is completely Yin or completely Yang and understanding this reality had made life easier since the beginning of time.

Just like nature has its Yin Yang, understanding the nature of things in the Web and, above all, understanding that not everything is black or white and that not everything is "forever", or that there are no absolute certainties, makes the lives of Website "owners" a lot easier, since many times they have to make decisions without absolute certainties.

At SRP Interactive, we have often felt frustrated due to the limitations of the Internet, because things didn't work the way we expected them to or due to changing technologies. We have been right many times … and wrong many others.

The 222 Tips that we have chosen to include in this book are a summary of the experience gained by working and doing, with the frequent help of own clients, from whom we also have learned.

Working on the Internet is about teamwork; and the interaction of the Yin and Yang forces is essential. Through our own experience, we have learned that a Website entirely created by designers does not work, literally; just as one created entirely by programmers looks awful, does not convey anything and therefore, doesn't work either. In order to start achieving acceptable results on the Internet, we need at least, the interaction of these two groups of professionals.

We hope these Tips are useful to you and that they help you understand the Yin Yang of the Web, to achieve better results in business online.

Sebastián Pincetti and Silvina Rodriguez Picaro

"

# "If it's not on the Internet, it simply doesn't exist."

## Generation Y*

* The demographic cohort that follows Generation X, which includes those born between 1982 and 1992. These are people that use the Internet on a daily basis, and spend a minimum of 20 hours per week online. The digital natives are those who were born towards the end of the last millennium and essentially as of the 21st century, when digital technology was already fully installed.

Computers, cell phones, tablets and MP3 players are natural elements to their environment and they cannot imagine life without them, almost in the same way that previous generations could not imagine life without electricity.

# DISCLAIMER

This book was published in 2012. By the time you finish reading this, there will surely be new technologies, new Websites, more statistics and other means of communication.

Some of the Tips will have been overcome by technology and at the same time, new challenges will have emerged, leading to new Tips. Yes, everything is changing too fast. The Internet is always in beta phase*.

Many of the Tips you will find in this book may seem contradictory. We could not help it. That's the nature of the Internet.

* Experimental phase

"

"The Internet is becoming the town square for the global village of tomorrow."

**Bill Gates**

# INTRODUCTION

**"222 Tips for doing Business on the Internet"** is a set of guidelines we have learned from working with our clients since the first days of the Internet. We want to share these Tips with our readers so that their online businesses have a simpler and more prosperous life.

This is a book for anyone interested in doing business on the Internet, or working on a Website, either in a company or in an advertising agency, a public relations consulting company, or simply for entrepreneurs who want to make the most of their resources minimizing the mistakes.

Nowadays, having a quality Website is essential for every business. Whether it's for a small shop, a small sized company or a global corporation, everyone needs a Website and an online strategy. Furthermore, from an entrepreneur to a musician or from an artist to a rock & roll band, it is necessary to have a solid presence on the Internet to be able to achieve your goals.

Not having a Website—or at least some presence on the Internet—will not only make it more difficult for people to find you, but will also send the wrong message. Just picture the following: What do you think when someone gives you a business card with an e-mail address ending in "@hotmail.com"?

We wrote this book with the "owner" or the "person responsible" for a Website in mind, or even more so, with the person in charge of carrying out the online business strategy in mind. This is the person who has to make decisions that will affect your business at times without having all the tools at hand.

**"222 Tips for doing Business on the Internet"** is about the nature of life online and it will be useful to you so that you can evaluate the pros and cons of every decision, both when it comes to leading a project as well as when it comes to somehow taking part in it.

It is the same need that many of our clients have. For they have inspired us to write these 222 Tips. We hope you find them useful.

**The Authors**

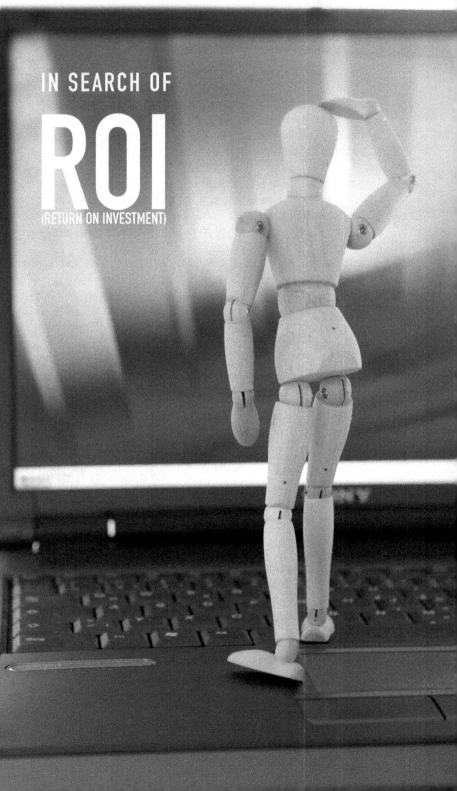

IN SEARCH OF

# ROI
(RETURN ON INVESTMENT)

# 1: THE NATURE OF THE INTERNET

Truly understanding the nature of the Internet will save you a lot of time, money and effort.

It is a medium that has its own codes, frontiers, strengths and weaknesses. Know what to expect from it and how to achieve your goals.

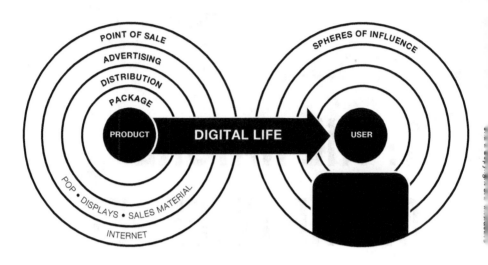

The chart shows how nowadays, digital life demands the product to have at least one digital component from its very conception until user reception. From the package itself to the Point of Sale there is some digital component that gets connected to the user and somehow influences him/her. From the simple bar code to chips that can identify if the cold chain has been broken at a certain point of the distribution, or the possibility of relating a certain credit card to certain purchasing habits. This is not science fiction, but a reality that is already part of our lives. This trend will be growing in the future and the traceability of the product will be complete.

# WHAT IT'S ALL ABOUT

Everything happens very fast on the Internet ... The user is always one click away from leaving your Website. The faster we help him/her understand what it's all about, the better.

**1** › **First impressions count**

The user channel surfs through Websites, just as he/she does when watching TV. This is why it is necessary to have a Website that works properly, has fast-loading pages, and is clear and appealing from the content to the design perspective. There is never a second chance to create a good impression. Much less if it's online.

**2** › **The user has to be able to understand in seconds what the Website is about**

If your message is not clear, the user is going to leave your Website immediately. He/she won't waste time trying to understand what you meant to do or say. The site needs to offer concrete reasons as to why the user should stay and it must do it fast!

**3** › **Be as specific as possible**

Whenever you work on the Internet, always bear in mind your objective. Less is more. If you have many diverse topics to develop, it's better to think of developing several related Websites. This is better than creating only one Website that tries to meet all the objectives at the same time. The "*one size fits all*" simply doesn't work on the Internet.

## Less is More

## 4 › Page Titles I

The title is the first thing that appears on the browser when the page is loading. This is why it is necessary to give each page a different title, to briefly describe the contents the user will find. On the other hand, if a user has several tabs open on the same browser, it will be difficult to make him/her return to the page without a descriptive and appealing title.

## 5 › Message and Target

Before starting, ask yourself what story you want to tell, and what dialogue you want to entail with your target audience.

## 6 › Website's purpose

It may seem like a simple question, but we have often seen that the answer is not that simple. Establish what the Website's purpose is as regards to the target audience, and as you move forward with the Website, ask yourself if what you are doing responds to that mission.

## 7 › Don't assume that the only way to enter the Website is through the homepage

Users can enter the Website either through search engines or through a specific link that has been sent to them or through any other webpage and not necessarily through the homepage. Surfing the Internet is never linear and many times it is unpredictable, unless you have a Website made entirely on Flash (if that's the case, read the book until the end and draw your own conclusions). This is why users need to quickly know what the Website is about, regardless of which page they enter.

## 8 › Accept that not everything is under your control

The way in which your Website is visualized not only depends on you, but also on users. The installed software, the type of connection and the network they are on all play an essential part. Just as an example, icons or messages that were not developed on your Website will pop up many times, like for instance, flags are automatically added next to the phone numbers if users have Skype installed on their computers.

## 9 › Ongoing Investment

Don't imagine that your Website is a one time investment. Maintaining a Website is like maintaining a store, it needs to be updated and kept interesting so that people keep coming back. The Website is alive and if it is updated on a continous basis, it has more chances of success than a Website that doesn't.

# 10 BASIC ACTIONS FOR THE WEBSITE'S ONGOING MAINTENANCE

❑ **Measure Traffic / Statistics**

❑ **Do SEO (Search Engine Optimization)**

❑ **Give Signs of Life***

❑ **Update the Information**

❑ **Verifify that the Links are Active**

❑ **Monitor the Online Reputation**

❑ **Monitor the Actions of the Competitors**

❑ **Verify it Functions properly with New Technologies**

❑ **Verify the Hosting is the Website always online?**

❑ **Evaluate Results: does it meet the objectives?**

Chart: Copyright SRP Interactive

* Send an automatic answer to queries confirming e-mail reception and reply within 24 hr.

# A GOOD NAME...

A good name says it all, and it helps the user to quickly understand what the Website is about.

### 10 › Choose a name to keep the domain short

Try not to have the name exceed the 12 characters (excluding the www. and the extension). The shorter the name, the better it is! You can verify if the domains are taken at: *www.whois.com.* Make sure the domain is under your name or your company name; never leave it at the hands of third parties.

### 11 › Choose a name related to your brand or activity

Choose a domain that is accurate or that contains the name of your brand, company or activity. Or, better yet, choose a domain related to your subject matter. This can be very powerful because it can position you as leader in your category on the Internet.

### 12 › Make sure that your domain is pronounceable in different languages

Try to use neutral words that are easy to pronounce in several languages.

### 13 › Try to make it memorable

Choose a name that is easy to remember and spell: this is an essential trait. Avoid names in which the same two vowels or two consonants are together (e.g.: advertising group, interactive entertainment or organic company). Also avoid using acronyms or words that are difficult to spell.

### 14 › Avoid acronyms (unless they are memorable)

Acronyms only should be used when they belong to established names, preferably if they are very popular or memorable ones (UNICEF, IBM, KPMG, and SRP). Avoid creating acronyms that users won't be able to remember or write.

**15** › **The message in the extension** (.com, .edu, .org,
**or the country's extension)**
The extension says a lot about the Website. Think of how you want to be
perceived (globally, in the local market, as a nonprofit organization, an
academic organization, among others) and then choose your extension.
If it is a global brand and with a budget, don't doubt it: register the
extension in every country where your brand has a presence. Do not
leave the open possibility for others to use your name.

**16** › **Be present on Social Networks**
With the same criterion as in the previous Tip, don't leave an open
door for someone else to use your brand on the most important Social
Networks. Reserve your place on social networks compatible with your
brand. For example:

| | |
|---|---|
| - YouTube | - Sónico |
| - Facebook | - Orkut |
| - Twitter | - SurveyMonkey |
| - SlideShare | - WebEx |
| - LinkedIn | - Eventsbot |
| - MySpace | - Gotomeeting |

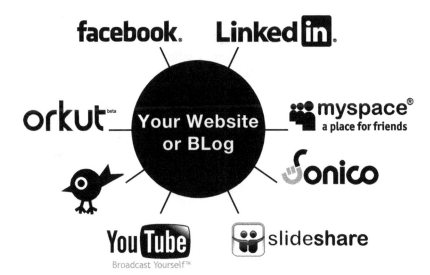

Stay up to date, the list will surely keep growing. All the efforts made
by the company regarding social networks should be integrated. The
Website or Blog should function as the central hub.

## 17 › **Be multidomain**

Have several domains that point to the same Website. This will undoubtedly benefit you by capturing more traffic.

## 18 › **The user can make mistakes when typing**

If you are going to use a name that can generate potential spelling problems, it is a good idea to register all the domains that may look alike or generate confusion and redirect the traffic to the correct domain. This way you will capture the greatest possible traffic. For example, the Marriott Hotels (*www.marriott.com*) have a considerable problem with people recalling the proper spelling. Thus, they have bought all the possible names and combinations and they automatically redirect the user to their Website to avoid this problem.

## 19 › **Try for the domain name to have some of the keywords**

Another good idea is for the domain name to include some of the keywords that users will enter into search engine queries. Just as an example, if your business is home security, it would be convenient to register: *www.homewatchers.com*.

## 20 › **Don't use special characters**

Avoid including numbers, dashes, underscores, and letters that are not in the English language, articles or conjunctions in the address you choose. Try to be as simple as possible. It is proven that users tend to forget about dashes and special characters.

## 21 › **Make sure the domain name has positive connotations**

What is positive in one language may not be positive in another. Do the exercise of finding a name that is positive in all the possible languages.

Domain Name ◄──► Telephone Number

≠                           ≠

Hosting ◄──► Telephone Service
(ISP)                 (CARRIER)

This simple chart shows a parallelism between a Website and the telephone service, comparing the domain name with the telephone number and the hosting (provided by the ISP) with the telephone service (provided by the Carrier). If you want to change hosting you can do so without changing domain name. Likewise, you can change telephone company without changing your number.

# A GOOD IMAGE

A well cared for and efficient brand image is the first step to achieving a quality Website. Everything counts when it comes to looking professional. The logo, the choice of color, the type set, the icons and other brand identifiers say a lot about the quality of the Website.

**22** › **Use the power of the tagline***

Through an accurate and succinct sentence, you will be able to reinforce the chosen name for your Website with its action and objective areas. This is how LG says "Life's Good" (*www.lg.com*), Epson proposes to "Exceed your vision" (*www.epson.com*), and at SRP Communication & Brand Design, we communicate: "Ideas that Work" (*www.srpdesign.com*). Other interesting examples are those of Office Depot (*www.officedepot.com*) with its slogan "Taking care of business" and Vista Print (*www.vistaprint.com*) with its "Best Printing. Best Practice".

A good tagline is the key for the user to quickly grasp what your brand and your Website are all about!

* (See chart on page 30)

# WEB BRANDING

Necessary elements to
## connect to the user

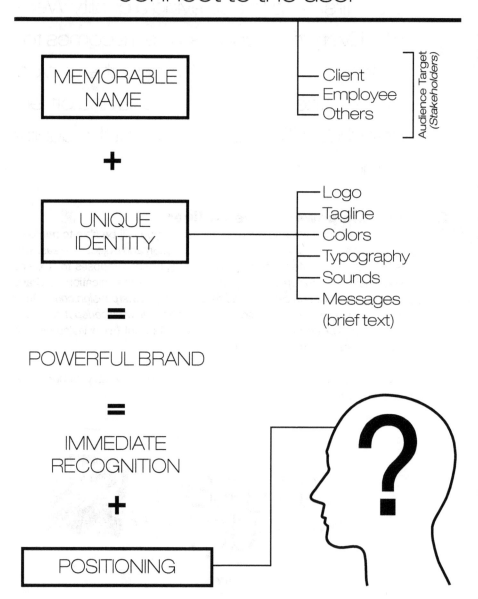

MEMORABLE
NAME

— Client
— Employee
— Others

Audience Target
*(Stakeholders)*

**+**

UNIQUE
IDENTITY

— Logo
— Tagline
— Colors
— Typography
— Sounds
— Messages
(brief text)

**=**

POWERFUL BRAND

**=**

IMMEDIATE
RECOGNITION

**+**

POSITIONING

# PROTECT YOUR WEBSITE

Your Website is public and can be visited both, by friends and foes (hackers, competitors, robots, etc.). Protecting your Website is as important as protecting any asset of your organization.

## 23 › Protect of your Website through a Trademark

It's a good idea to use a name that can be registered in the corresponding category (®, ™), because of its characteristics.

(See chart on page 32)

## 24 › Protect your e-mail address

Publish your e-mail address as an image and not as text. This way you will avoid SPAM in your e-mail, since robots cannot read images yet. Another option is to generate a contact form. Always evaluate the cost-benefit ratio between the SPAM risk and the benefit of allowing users to do copy-paste on the e-mail when they want to contact you through this means.

## 25 › Include a Legal Disclosure

It is important that your Website have a legal disclosure or notice to specify responsibilities. In the case of photographs of products on sale, for instance, it is possible for colors or format to differ from the merchandise that users will buy. This is why it is important for users to know this in order to avoid false expectations.

## 26 › Include a Privacy Policy

Briefly describe how you protect the privacy of your client or user.

### 27 › **Include a Copyright Notice**

The Website is part of your intellectual property. Don't forget to include a footnote specifying the copyright and date.

### 28 › **Domain name and brand**

Before buying a domain name, make sure that it isn't the trademark of another company. You can verify it on the Internet:

United States: *www.uspto.gov*          Brazil: *www.inpi.gov.br*
Argentina: *www.inpi.gov.ar*          Chile: *www.inapi.cl*
Spain: *www.oepm.es*          Colombia: *www.sic.gov.co*

# BRAND PROTECTION

## =

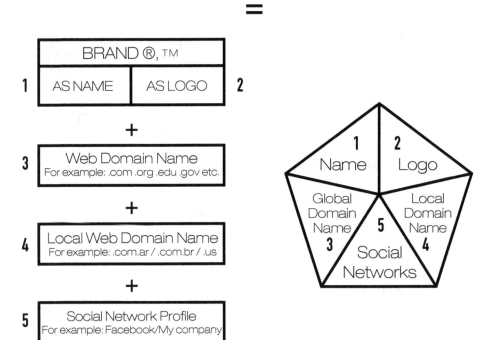

The chart shows all the registers to take into account to protect the Website's brand. It suggests registering the brand as name and logo, as well as the local and global domain names, and the social network profiles compatible with the brand.

Chart: Copyright SRP Interactive

# CONTENT

The Website's content is the most important reason why users visit it. It is also the reason why they stay longer and why they will return it, if they decide to do so…*

**29 › Write thinking about the Web**

What you write will be read from a screen and will rarely be printed. Keep this in mind at all times. A huge amount of text is a bad experience, is intimidating, boring and difficult to read. Write for Websites, not for printed media. Everything that helps users quickly find what they are looking for and stay in the Website is welcome. Most of the content published on the Internet has a format that is hardly suitable for the medium. Texts must be short and accurate. It is essential that they be identified at a glance and, above all, that they are to the point. Avoid the blah, blah, blah.

**30 › Don't write long paragraphs**

Long paragraphs are especially intimidating to read on a computer screen. Use bullet points and short paragraphs. This way you will keep the reader's attention on the screen. (See Tip 29)

* (See chart on page 34)

# FACTORS THAT MAKES THE USER RETURN TO THE WEBSITE

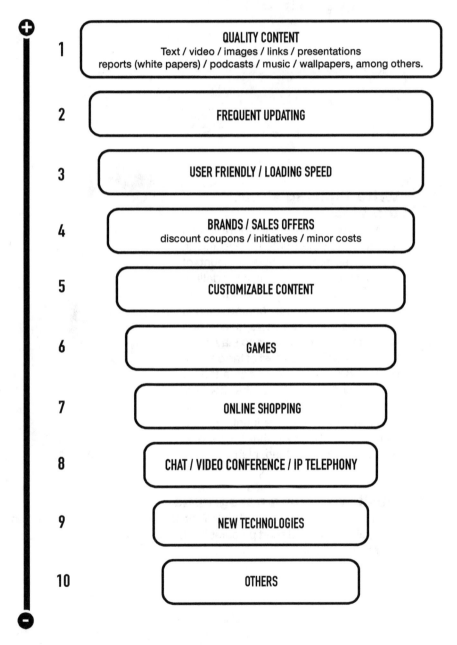

1. **QUALITY CONTENT**
Text / video / images / links / presentations
reports (white papers) / podcasts / music / wallpapers, among others.

2. **FREQUENT UPDATING**

3. **USER FRIENDLY / LOADING SPEED**

4. **BRANDS / SALES OFFERS**
discount coupons / initiatives / minor costs

5. **CUSTOMIZABLE CONTENT**

6. **GAMES**

7. **ONLINE SHOPPING**

8. **CHAT / VIDEO CONFERENCE / IP TELEPHONY**

9. **NEW TECHNOLOGIES**

10. **OTHERS**

The chart shows the most important factors that make the user revisit the Website, in descending order. Quality content is undoubtedly the main factor that enables achieving this objective.

## 31 › **Establish levels of reading**

Website readers are used to scanning through the page to decide if they stay or not. This is why it is necessary to organize the Website at different levels, to make the reading easier and extend the stay in a friendly way.

Reading from a screen is more difficult than reading from printed material. This is why establishing levels of reading (headline, lead, bullet points, etc.) acquires more relevance, especially if it's read over a smart phone.

---

# Very important

## Less important

### Not so important

Additional Information

---

## 32 › **Make it crawlable**

Make sure that all your Website can be scanned by the users (who are used to quickly scanning the information of the webpage), as well as crawlable by the most popular search engines on the Internet (Google, Yahoo!, Bing*, among others).

## 33 › **Eliminate useless content** (Use hyperlinks)

Even though it is important for each webpage to have the right amount of content so as to not intimidate users, the Internet has the great advantage that there are no limits to the amount of content you can add. You can add everything you consider necessary. By using links and dividing the text into new pages, the reading will be more fluent and friendly. This is why it is necessary to segment each portion of information you wish to provide through links to new pages. This way, you avoid making the experience of users surfing through your Website a boring one. (See Tip 119)

---

\* Bing is the search engine launched by Microsoft in June 2009. It is promoted as a smart search engine, that helps the decision making process. According to its description, it searches and organizes the answers needed by users so that they can make faster and more informed decisions.

# CONTENT MANAGEMENT

## Keys for Success in the Digital Era

**BE DIGITAL**

Volvo Drive for Life (Virtual Test Drive for XBOX)
www.century21.com
www.cite-sciences.fr

In spite of being a brick and mortar organization

**1  TELL A STORY** ►
www.ted.com
www.pharmacyforme.org
www.ashtonscoolpix.com

**2  INVITE TO PLAY** ►
www.americasarmy.com
www.bk.com
www.disneylatino.com

**3  BE CREATIVE** ►
www.ray-ban.com
www.giraffe.net
www.tijuanaflats.com

**4  BE INNOVATIVE** ►
www.bugaboo.com
www.weightwatchers.com
www.theaxeeffect.com

**5  BE CATCHY** ►
www.facebook.com
www.twitter.com
www.youtube.com

**6  LOOK FOR ALLIES**
Cobranding ►
nike+apple
The biggest looser+Nintendo
www.lacasae.com

**7  BE SOCIABLE** ►
www.linkedin.com
www.baeblemusic.com
www.brahma.com.br

**8  BE USEFUL** ►
www.eatbetteramerica.com
www.ebay.com
www.emaservicetips.com

**9  BE TRANSPARENT** ►
www.mystarbucksidea.com
www.jetblue.com
www.geico.com

**10  THINK GREEN** ►
www.willyoujoinus.com
www.greenpeace.org
www.philips.com

**11  BE PORTABLE**
Smartphones, Tablets ►
www.freshdirect.com
www.ole.com.ar
www.benjerry.com

**12  LIVE 24/7** ►
www.amazon.com
www.miamiherald.com
www.wired.com

Chart: Copyright SRP Interactive

## 34 › Give users a good reason to visit your Website and stay there

Be brief and clear. A few words that make sense—write useful things. This is better than a bunch of irrelevant sentences your visitors will barely read ("about us…", "our mission..."). Useless wording will cause users to leave out of boredom.

## 35 › About us (About the company)

Briefly describe your history, your abilities and objectives. Say why your company or organization is different from the others in a clear and concise way. Stand out from your competitors without naming them.

## 36 › If you have to be too technical make a glossary

Including certain technical terminology (or in another language) is sometimes useful to fascinate many users. It distinguishes the Website, it shows quality and know how, but it also eliminates the possibility of being found by those who don't know the name of what they are looking for.

Take this into account all the time and use simple terms that coexist with the more sophisticated terminology: this way, possible non specialist clients will find you.

## 37 › You attitude

**(Always use the second person)**

Try to use "you" as much as you can, instead of using "I" or "we". The content always needs to be created keeping users in mind. Focus on speaking from the users' benefits and not from the pride of "I" or "we" because it simply won't work.

## 38 › Include FAQs (Frequently Asked Questions)

Offer users frequently asked questions with their corresponding answers. Don't make them waste time and don't waste your time by making them ask something already asked by most people who visit your Website.

## 39 › **Avoid introductions**

Having to wait for something to load or having to watch and wait for an animated movie to finish during several seconds without knowing what the Website has to offer, drives users away, in spite of the efforts made in the Website's development. It's not enough to put "skip intro", it is also essential to convey everything that will be found in the Website in one second.

## 40 › **The Website intro**

Just like an effective movie trailer, a good intro generates curiosity in users and makes them want to know more. On the contrary, a bad intro drives them away.
The intro should:
- Inform and entertain
- Respect the bandwidth
- Always include the "skip intro" option
- Not be boring nor too long
- Not include unnecessary information
- Allow users to turn off the audio, if any
- Convey what the Website is about
And above all, make sure it loads fast!

(See Tip 103)

## 41 › **Develop useful applications for users**

If you can include useful applications, don't doubt it: this is the best place to do so. Some of these ideal applications may include calculators that figure out monthly installments, how to optimize materials or how to save energy, to name a few.

 **Fertility Calculator**

Trying to get pregnant? Our fertility and ovulation calculator can tell you the best days to try to conceive. It can even tell you your baby's possible due date! To determine when you're most likely to conceive, enter the first day of your last menstrual period:

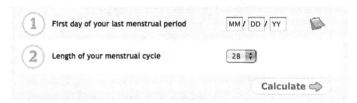

Image: www.parenting.com/fertility-calculator.

Read 222
Tips...
Review
statistics
Use the
SRP
Interactive
checklist
Call SRP
Interactive
Visit
www.222tips.biz
Establish
objectives!
Measure
results
Conduct
testing
Understand
the web
glossary

## 42 › **Use of visual metaphors**

On the Internet, metaphors help us transfer the real-world experiences of users into cyberspace.

Use a metaphor if:
- It is appropriate for the brand or product
- It makes navigation easier
- Improves the user's experience
- It doesn't sound far fetched
- It doesn't outshine the brand

A typical example of a good visual metaphor is the shopping cart used by many Websites that sell products online.

## 43 › **Help users with a Checklist**

Provide user-friendly tools, helpful for the user's activity. For instance, if your site is about baby care, make a list for parents, so that they don't forget to take any important items their baby may need whenever they go out.

## 44 › **Wallpapers**

Create wallpapers that are appealing for users, call their attention so that they want to download them and put them on their computers.

## 45 › **Use your own photographs or purchase stock photography**

Make sure you have the rights to publish the photos you put on your Website and control that it is for as long as you need.

(See Tip 142)

## 46 › **Use the power of surveys**

Ask users about their opinion regarding your Website and how they think you can improve it to satisfy their navigating experience. Also keep your Website updated with small surveys that allow users to compare their opinions to those of other users.

Image: cnn.com

# WORK METHODOLOGY

We could spend hours talking about this point in particular, but we will only provide details of Tips we consider to be essential.

## 47 › Planning

It is convenient to dedicate time to planning the Website's functionalities. Doing so requires paying attention to all the details beforehand, so later you can be ready for Website deployment. Working without a defined plan is costly, inefficient and often frustrating. Imagine constructing a building without a blueprint. Planning allows you to be ahead of the game. Better safe than sorry.

## 48 › Details

Don't pay too much attention to details. Although they may be important and necessary to look good, dedicating too much time to them or having this exclusive dedication holding the Website back from being online on time, may be counterproductive. Bear in mind that many of these details will be overlooked by users. It is part of the Web's nature, in which—more than ever—time is money.

## 49 › First do it, then change it

Timing on the Internet is essential. Experience indicates that it is better to have a working Website than an impeccable one, or to never even implement something in the search of unreachable perfection. Working on the Internet has the great advantage that it can be modified all the time. Therefore: why use the logic of working on printed media, which cannot be modified once it's delivered? In a nutshell: Just do it. Time is money...

## 50 › Change the way you work

Think of your work as never finished or needing improvement on a daily basis. Ask yourself how many webpages from competitors appear everyday. This shows you that you cannot just sit on your hands.

## 51 › **Static or dynamic?**

When you're thinking of designing a Website, this is probably the first question you should ask yourself. So you should be able to answer it before the first drafts are made. The words "static" or "dynamic" may lead to confusion and many people think a Website is dynamic just because it has Flash or videos or animated GIFs that seem to move on the screen. Generally speaking, if the Website has e-commerce or frequently changing information (such as a newspaper Website), it is undoubtedly dynamic. In other words, it has variable information that responds to a database. If the Website remains unmodified for a certain amount of time, it won't be necessary to invest in making it dynamic, at least at the beginning. The following chart will help you understand the concept and will be very useful when it comes to making decisions that fit your needs.

| ▶ WEBSITE | ▶ STATIC | ▶ DYNAMIC |
|---|---|---|
| Accepts Flash or Animated GIFs | Yes | Yes |
| Accepts Images or Video | Yes | Yes |
| Accepts Text | Yes | Yes |
| Accepts Internal Search | No | Yes |
| Uses Databases | No | Yes |
| Visualized webpage | What is developed is what is seen | It's a template with a code that takes information from a database |
| Number of Pages | 1 per product shown | 1 for all the products shown |
| Page Layout Maintenance | If something wants to be changed in all the pages, all the pages have to be modified | The template is modified |
| Update of information on webpages | To modify the information on Webpages, knowledge of webpage development is required. | A Content Manager is required to modify the information on Webpages (See Tip 187) |
| Type of Access to modify webpages | FTP (File Transfer Protocol) | Internet browser |
| Requirements of the Hosting Server | Simple | More powerful and with more memory requirement |
| Advisable | For webpages with few updates and few products/services | For webpages with many updates and many products/services |
| Online Sales | Not Advisable | Advisable |
| Initial Cost | Low ⊖ | High ⊕ |
| Maintenance and Update Cost | High ⊕ | Low ⊖ |
| Update Speed | Slow (generally done by a third party during working hours) | Immediate (done by the person responsible for the company at any time and place) |

### 52 › **Look for professional assistance**
The tools are accessible to everyone and anyone can design a webpage but only a webpage designed by professionals can offer the results you need for your business to succeed.

# THE POSITIVE LOOP

## Work process: from idea to continuous improvement

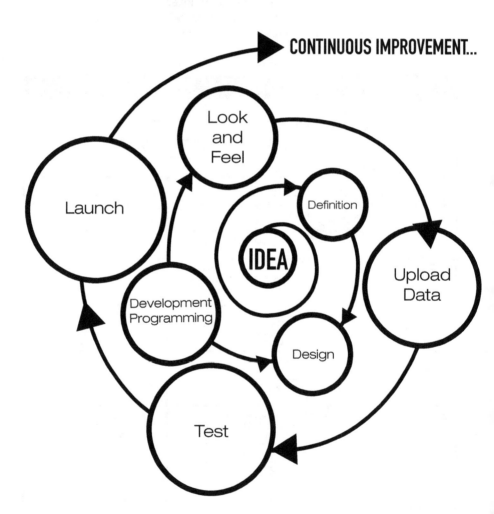

The chart shows the work on the Internet as a positive upward spiral that never ends, looking for continuous improvement.

Chart: Copyright SRP Interactive

## 53 › **Work in a Multi-disciplinary Team**

Nowadays, working on a successful Website is comparable to working on the set of a Hollywood movie. It's the result of the combined work of an interdisciplinary team, with a lot of talent and few hours of sleep. A list that is sure to grow as the industry becomes more professional:

- Usability experts
- Technology experts
- Web Developers
- Designers
- Advertisers
- Public Relations (PR) Experts
- Content Generators

- Infographics Experts
- Writers
- Editors
- Photographers
- Musicians
- SEO experts
- Community Managers
- Digital Marketing Experts

# 2: VISIBILITY
## (OR HOW GET THEM
## TO FIND ME)

Getting your target audience to find
your Website is a task that requires
special expertise. This is the case both
in terms of traditional off-line promotion,
as well as for promotion on the Web,
where search engines play a key role,
as does online advertising through banners
or other more sophisticated means.

# ONLINE MARKETING

All efforts are important when it comes to promoting your Website online. Make sure it can be found by search engines and register it in directories. Know all the secrets!

## 54 › Use text-based navigation

The text-based navigation is not only much faster, but also allows users who have turned "off" images and as well as those using smartphones (iPhone, Blackberry, Android, among others)—a growing market—to navigate without problems. You may use some of the online tools that allow you to test what your Website looks like on smartphones and on some of the most popular browsers.

## 55 › Make sure that users can search the entire Website

When choosing the technology for your Website, make sure it can be indexed by search engines. This allows your site to be found by users, not only the first page, but any of them. It is essential that the Website be crawlable if you want results.

## 56 › Use descriptive URLs

Using simple and easy-to-read URL structures will not only make the user understand what the Website is about before accessing it, but will further improve how it ranks on search engines.

2: VISIBILITY | 49

## 57 › Be sure to put the anchor text instead of the links

When the goal is for someone to click on a link, it is essential to put a relevant text, instead of detailing how to write the link itself. It's far more user-friendly and leads to better results on search engines.

## 58 › Make sure all images have labels

This serves a dual purpose. First, it is beneficial when it comes to search engines indexing and ranking the webpage. This is because search engines can't read what is inside an image, but can read what is inside the "ALT" label. Secondly, it helps users to define if they want to wait or not for the image to finish loading—in case it's taking too long.

## 59 › Page titles II

It is very common to see a Website in which all pages have the same title, or have a default one created by the program used to build the site (TITLE tag). Keep in mind that the title is a very important component used by search engines when performing a search. (See Tip 4)

## 60 › Don't use links created with JavaScript*

Search engines cannot find links generated through JavaScript (causing pages not to be indexed by search engines). In addition, links made with JavaScript often create problems for the user when navigating the site and, even worse, will not allow navigation on smartphones.

## 61 › Don't use hidden text

All text which is identical in color to the page's background color cannot be read by the naked eye, and is thereby hidden. This is a technique that is used to overload a webpage with keywords. Search engines don't like hidden text because it is something that deceives them. They assume it is used to improve indexing.

## 62 › Register with all possible search engines and directories

If you want to be visible, be sure to register with as many search engines and directories as possible. The more search engines and directories that link to you, the more popular you'll be and the higher the chances of being found. Don't forget to have presence on Wikipedia.

* JavaScript is a scripting language based on objects. It is primarily used integrated into Web browsers and enables the development of improved user interfaces and dynamic webpages.

# OPTIMIZATION OF ONLINE ADVERTISING

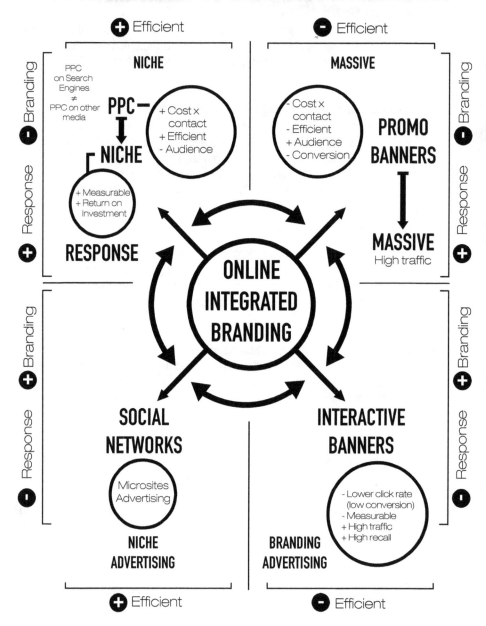

The chart shows four types of online advertising, highlighting strengths and weaknesses. It divides forms of advertising that are more effective at generating a response from those that are more effective at generating brand image (branding). At the same time, it suggests the interrelation between these forms. For example, PPC (Pay per click) when used in search engines is the most efficient resource in order to generate response, but is weaker when it comes to increasing the audience, because it originates from the specific need of the user instead of his/her impulse, as in the case of interactive banners.

Chart: Copyright SRP Interactive

## 63 › Link exchange section

In order to be popular not only must your Website be registered with as many search engines and directories as possible, but must also be linked from other Websites. This requires having a link exchange section. Make sure links are reciprocal and not only from your Website to others.

## 64 › Don't put links to banned sites

If you place links from your Website, either by exchanging links or because you want to show some specific information, make sure it is not to a banned Website. And remember to check this regularly! Google, for example, is very strict with this issue. And if you wish to have visibility, you cannot afford to be left out of Google.

## 65 › Choose your keywords well

Use tools to help you choose keywords for your Website. Use free tools, such as those offered by Adwords* and Seomoz.org—which will help you choose the best keywords used by users when making a search.

## 66 › Use keywords in the text

When developing the site, keep in mind that not only is it important to place keywords in the Metatags, but also on the main body text on the page.

---

* AdWords, the auction-based system run by Google to sell ads on search engines is probably the most successful business idea in the history of advertising. It reports an estimated 20 billion dollars in annual revenue. Source: Clarín (Argentine daily newspaper).

## 67 › Beware of Flash

The Flash is the enemy of SEO (Search Engine Optimization). Everything inside Flash files is invisible to search engines. A Website based solely on Flash is very nice ... but it will not be found. Only use Flash when you need to do something that HTML cannot do (games, video player, special animations) and make sure that is only part of the Website, not all of it. (See Myths about SEO)

(See chart on page 91)

## 68 › Contact Information

Take advantage of every possible way to help the user make contact with you in the virtual world and the real world.
- Make a printer-friendly interactive map with their physical location.
- Explain how to arrive (by car, public transportation, from airport) and where to find parking.
- Publish your e-mail, phone number and address.
- And anything else that can be used to make life easier for the user.

(See Tip 24)

## 69 › Don't use Frames

Frames make Web indexing very difficult and therefore, the visibility of the Website is jeopardized. Additionally, bear in mind that if someone wants to put a webpage that is inside a frame as "favorite", it will be very challenging to achieve, unless that person is an advanced user. Finally, it is important to know that there are browsers that do not support this technology.

## 70 › Know the PageRank of your pages

Each site has a score (PageRank), which is the way Google determines how important the page is. It does not rank the Website as a whole, but each page within it separately. So every page within a Website has a different PageRank. When displaying search results, Google combines PageRank with the text being queried, assigning priority to pages with a higher PageRank.

**Important:** Having a high PageRank does not mean having more visits than another site with a lower PageRank. Remember that this only works with the concept of page relevance. (See Myths about PageRank)

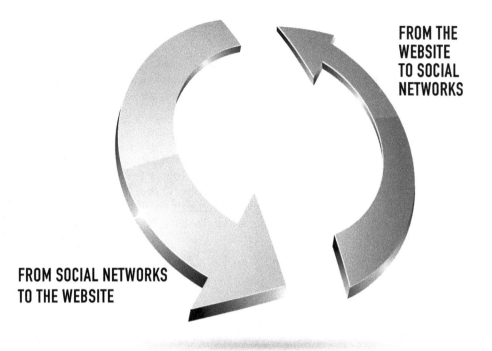

FROM THE
WEBSITE
TO SOCIAL
NETWORKS

FROM SOCIAL NETWORKS
TO THE WEBSITE

### 71 › Promoting on Social Networks

Just like the signature in e-mails, mentioning your Website on the social networks you use (LinkedIn, Facebook, MySpace, SlideShare, Twitter, etc.) can take people to your site. The goal is to generate traffic in two ways: from your Website to the Social Networks and vice versa. (See chart on page 82)

### 72 › Signature on e-mails

One trick as simple as placing the URL of your Website in the signature of e-mails of company staff members, can bring many curious users to your Website.

### 73 › E-mail Marketing

This is an effective and inexpensive means of promotion. When contacting the public via e-mail campaigns, it is of utmost importance to make clear who is sending the information and what that information is about (From and Subject). Beware: your e-mail should not get filtered as SPAM.*

---

* SPAM or junk mail refers to unsolicited, unwanted messages from an unknown sender. These are usually advertising messages, sent en masse. This type of message is most commonly sent via e-mail, but can also be sent through other media such as instant messaging or via mobile phone.

## 74 › **Languages I**

If you want to be found by people who speak a particular language, remember that your site must be in that language. Search engines do not translate when indexing and only find what is visible online.

## 75 › **Languages II**

Do not build a Website without an English version, unless you only want to work for your local audience. This is because the language of Shakespeare is the most used online. If your Website is only in a language which is not English, then half the world will not be able to read your Website. English works as a common code for most Internet users.

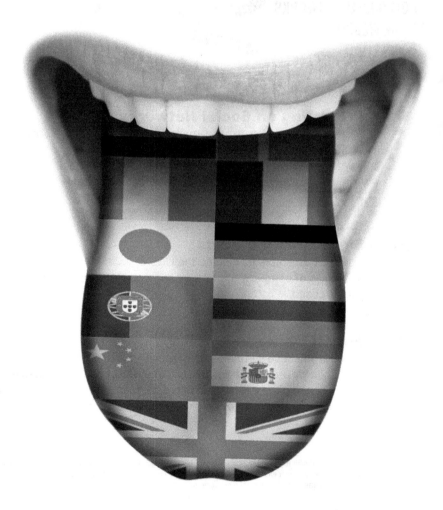

# OFFLINE MARKETING

A successful Website is not only promoted on the Internet, but also offline. Different channels from traditional advertising to public relations play a key role in creating the highly sought-after word-of-mouth...

## 76 › **Promote your Website online and offline**

As is the case with Yin and Yang, one type of promotion needs the other to achieve your ultimate goal: getting your target audience to navigate your Website and, above all, come back! Many well-known Websites have grown through traditional advertising and public relation campaigns. There is an endless list of Websites that advertise on broadcast or cable TV as well as the radio. If you want your Website to be known quickly, consider allocating into your budget, traditional advertising on broadcast and cable TV, public billboards, radio and print media.

The image shows a typical advertising billboard for GEICO near a highway in the United States. The famous slogan of the company: "Fifteen minutes could save you 15 percent or more on car insurance." is one of the most popular ones. Warren Buffet, chairman and CEO of Berkshire Hathaway, GEICO's holding company, said that if he could, he would invest 2 billion dollars in advertising per year. This is by no means a minor figure, although it is far from the $ 751 million dollars the company invested in advertising in 2007 (the date of the last known indicator).

# BUYING TRAFFIC

### 77 › **Buying Traffic**

Buying traffic through online advertising is a valid option if your product is very massive and you need to create viral behaviour. But this may also be an expensive and inefficient option. A banner in a high traffic Website (for example, a newspaper), if not well spent, may cost a fortune: billed monthly or even hourly. It is important to assess the results of the advertising schedule both from the branding perspective as well as from the sales generated by a specific action. Some campaigns are useful for brand image, but never translate into real sales. Don't get too excited, evaluate the cost-effectiveness before committing yourself to an advertising schedule.

### 78 › **Pay Per Click (PPC)**

It is a very interesting tool to drive traffic to your Website and capture the natural demand that your online product or service may have. It can also be very expensive and inefficient if it does not meet certain requirements:
- The more specific or segmented the site, the better the Conversion Rate on advertising*
- Make sure the IP is segmented to the regions where you wish to provide service**
- Set a daily spending limit
- Permanently monitor ROI
- Make sure you can meet the demand generated by the action.

There is no point investing in PPC if you then are unable to respond to the demand.

### 79 › **Restrict Pay Per Click (PPC)**

When hiring PPC, keep in mind that many Blogs—in order to finance themselves—ask their users to click on sponsored links. This generates a lot of useless traffic, since whoever clicks is not a potential prospect, genuinely interested. This of course, nevertheless still increases the cost per contact, and reduces the effectiveness of the action.

### 80 › **Online Advertising**

Putting banners on different Websites that have a high volume of visits is a good way to get traffic, provided that such Websites are related to your business.

* PPC conversion rate: the relationship between clicks and the number of times the ad was shown (impressions).

** Through the IP you can tell from which country your Website was accessed and in some countries from which state / province/city

# FROM CLICK TO CLIENT*

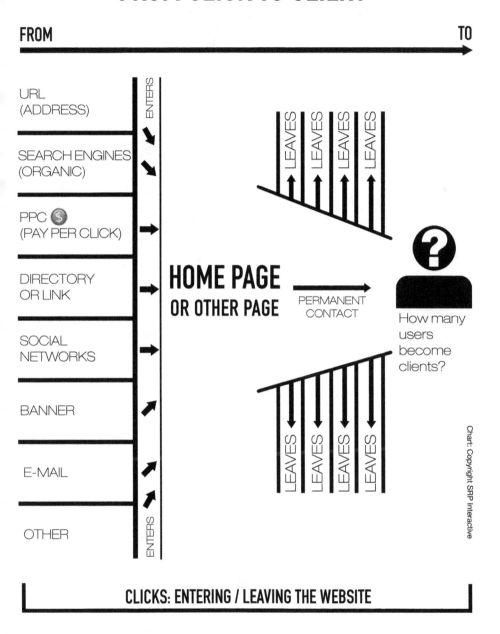

The chart shows the conversion rate dynamics, from the different ways in which users enter the Website and the various places where they access it, to the moment they leave, as well as users who finally "convert" by doing the desired action.

* Conversion also refers to the percentage of users who ultimately purchase or perform some desired action (e.g. subscribing to a mailing list), when visiting a Website.

"

It is much easier to increase
your Website's business by
improving your conversion
rate than by increasing traffic.

# BANNER CONVERSION

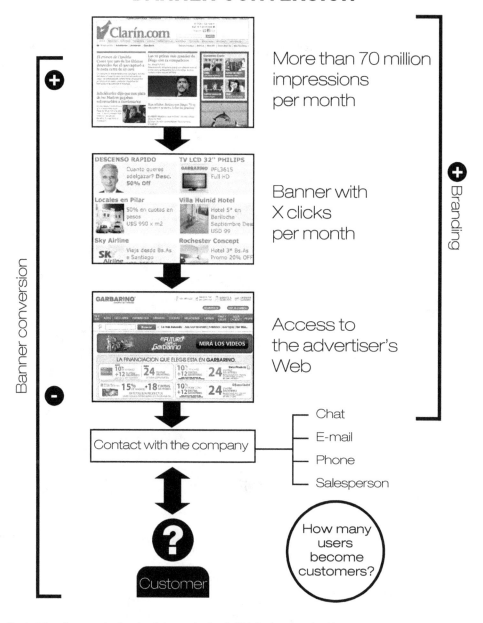

More than 70 million impressions per month

Banner with X clicks per month

Access to the advertiser's Web

Chat
E-mail
Phone
Salesperson

Contact with the company

How many users become customers?

Customer

Banner conversion

Branding

The chart shows the conversion dynamics of a banner placed on the Website of a major nationwide newspaper from the moment it was published to the action of clicking on the advertiser's Website to contact the company

* Images: Clarin.com
Clarín.com is one of the busiest sites in Argentina and online Spanish-language newspaper most consulted in Latin America, with 70 million impressions per month. Its holding company is Grupo Clarín.

Chart: Copyright SRP Interactive

# 3: USER

## (OR HOW TO PLEASE THE KING)

The user is the reason for everything
we do on the Internet. It's this person
who will determine the success
or failure of our work online. Satisfying the
user must be our main concern when
we pursue success on the Web.

"

"If there's one reason we have
done better than of our peers in the
Internet space over the last six years,
it is because we have focused like
a laser on customer experience,
and that really does matter, I think,
in any business. It certainly matters
online, where word of mouth
is so very, very powerful."

**Jeff Bezos**
CEO of Amazon.com

# GIVE THE USER CONTROL

**81 › If there is video or audio let the user decide when to play it**

If you want to show video or audio—except for the case of a band, a radio station, a television network, or a music Website—let users decide when to start playing the content, or if they even want to view it. Just think that this person may be in a company or public place, and not want to attract attention.

**82 › Offer the option of sending an e-mail contact via a form**

If you use the "mail to"* function—instead of a contact form—and the user is on a public computer and wants to contact the company through the page, he/she will not be able to. On public PCs, users cannot open the e-mail program, so it's essential to provide another option, like a form on the page itself.

**83 › Don't use fixed-size text or source**

Enable users to control the font size used on the Website through their browser. Let users choose how they want to view it. For this, define the size of sources in specific terms (em) instead of pixels (px).

(See Tip 145)

**84 › Don't sign up visitors without their consent**

Users must decide whether or not they wish to receive information. Never forget this rule because this behaviour can be considered invasive and put you into the unwanted category of "Spammer".

(See Tip 73)

* Automatically opens the user's default e-mail.

**85** › **Don't block the right button on the mouse**

Sometimes, for fear of having users copy text, images or for some other reason, Website owners block users from using the right button on the mouse. But it's pointless to do so. The user can copy the entire contents of a webpage by viewing the source code itself. Locking the right button on the mouse will only bother users who may need this feature for some reason.

**86** › **Accept that not everything is under your control II**

In Web design, it's not possible to tell the user how to navigate a Website. It doesn't work like a book, that depending on the language, can be read from right to left, left to right, top to bottom. You can only make suggestions, but the key is understanding that each user navigates differently.

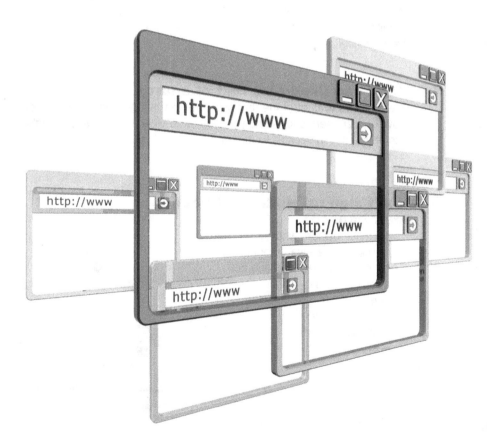

# DO NOT DISTURB THE USER (THE USER IS KING)

### 87 › Don't open new browser windows

When a new window opens automatically, the user might think: "More advertisement!", or perhaps consider it an error on the Website. Next thing you know, fatality strikes: the user closes all windows and abandons your Website.

### 88 › Pop Ups*

Don't bother the user with Pop Ups. Users are already very tired of these windows containing advertising that opens automatically. That is why in many cases they block this option. So if you do need to show something different, do it in the same window.

### 89 › Don't determine the size of the user's window

If you change users' screen size, you might inadvertently reconfigure other applications they are working on. Remember it is very possible that users may not know how to return to the previous configuration.

### 90 › Full Screen

Don't force users to use the full screen, since despite providing them a unique experience, may also prove to be annoying. Always let the user choose the form of visualization.

### 91 › Don't break navigation by overriding the back button

When users can't go back over their steps and/or get an error page, the feeling is that the Website doesn't work properly. This usually happens if you open a new window or use JavaScript links.

* A Pop Up is a small window that automatically pops up without the users' request when they access a webpage.

## 92 › Lead the conversation: Get to know your audience and value their opinion

The better you know your target audience, the easier you will get across to them. Be familiar with the Websites and Social Networks they visit and identify the type of contents they are interested in. Make the most of the 2.0 technology tools and lead the conversation about your brand or company by opening up new horizons, asking for the user's opinion and stimulating dialogue. Encourage the participation of key sectors of your company. This way you will be able to establish a genuine dialogue and therefore, a more credible one. (See Tip 46)

# PRINCIPLES OF ONLINE DIALOGUE

Research
Listen
Define Objectives
Optimize Tools
Generate Contents
Participate
Respond

## INFLUENCE

Users — Bloggers — Readers — Key stakeholders — Researchers

Journalists — Evaluators — Communicators — Groups

Others

Chart: Copyright SRP Interactive

## 93 › Don't ask for registration, unless it is necessary

Users only sign up if they think they will get something in return that is worth leaving their details. If it's necessary to sign up or get a subscription for something that is not important, it is likely that the user will leave and never return.

## 94 › Don't ask for personal information unless you need it

If you ask users who wish to sign up to answer questions about subjects that have no connection to what the site is about, they will either not come back to the Website because they believe your intention is only to get personal information or they will complete registration with useless or false information.

## 95 › "Install the following component, or you will not be able to navigate the Website..."

This message which often appears when entering a site, will usually really "scare users away", especially those who are not savvy or are afraid of technology. If the goal is for users to browse the site, you must be sure that they don't need to load anything extra to do so (for example, the latest Flash, ActiveX, Quicktime, Silverlight, etc.).

## 96 › Don't use cookies unless necessary

Many individual and company users, through their security policies, do not allow cookies* to be installed. In such a case, your Website would simply not work and their efforts would be wasted.

This is not a Cookie

* Cookies are small files which store information on a Website user's computer when first accessed. They are used to assign visitors an individual identification number that allows them to be recognized on subsequent visits and they recognize and remember user personal information and preferences.

### 97 › Don't Shout!

IT'S BEEN PROVEN THAT WORDS IN UPPER CASE ARE THE TEXT EQUIVALENT SHOUTING. Don't shout at users! They'll never forgive you.

### 98 › Uncomfortable or poorly designed forms

Avoid forms that request a lot of information at once. If you must meet multiple objectives, develop a specific form for every need. Make life easier for the user.

### 99 › If the link downloads a file, let users know!

When placing a link to a file, tell users what kind of file it is, and specify file size as well. Use icons and text links, a summary of the content, and finally, be sure to provide a link so users can, if necessary, install the plug-in to read the file.

### 100 › Don't have links that do not work

Continually check the links you have in your Website, especially if they point to other sites. These can be removed, changed, and so on. The credibility of your Website decreases if you have links that point to nowhere and give an error message.

### 101 › If users need to have an open port, let them know!

It's very common for some companies or users themselves to have certain ports* blocked. If you have a link to a Website that requires users to have certain ports open, notify it (for example, video cameras, Webmail, etc). If you don't do it, it will look like an error instead of a Firewall** issue. This is frequent when users are on a public network such as a cyber cafe, or a hotel, since these places normally block certain ports for security reasons.

---

* A logical port is a virtual link that enables the input and output of information from our computer. There are logical ports with different functionalities that enable programs to connect to our computer and transfer the information. If you are interested in knowing more about this topic, we recommend you to watch a video called Warriors of the Net on You Tube, which offers a simple and impeccable explanation.

** The Firewall is a filter (hardware or software) between the computer and the Network that limits possible connections through the logical ports.

### 102 › Website or webpage "under construction"

If part of your Website is not ready yet, don't upload it or a put menu for it. Only show the part of the Website that has been finished. Why tell everyone there's a webpage you haven't had time to finish yet?

### 103 › Slow loading webpages

Don't assume that everybody has fast Internet access and that users will be able to visualize your webpages, despite their file size. Remember that many times users share networks with other people or are downloading files or listening to music online at the same time. Keep in mind that more and more users are increasingly getting online from a mobile phone. This is why it's very important to use the ALT or TITLE attributes. Remember that the smaller the file size the better the experience! (See Tips 4 and 58)

### 104 › Inadequate image enlargement

It's common to include small images with the function that automatically enlarges them whenever users roll the mouse over them. It's necessary for users to know that the image will become larger, so that they can be the ones making the decision to do so.

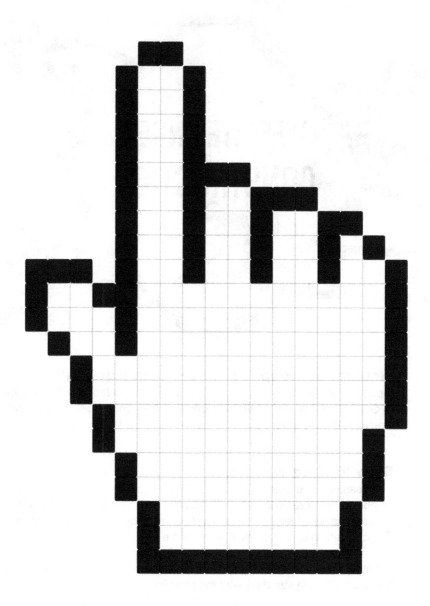

### 105 › **Don't mask your links** (Link cloaking)

A link shouldn't be masked with a name that points to another place when users click on it. This will be perceived negatively by users used to detecting such deceiving practices. An example of this is when users receive spam from an alleged bank, asking them to confirm the password and when clicking on it—instead of going where the link says—it takes them to another site.

### 106 › Webpages enemies of printers

It's not common for users to print webpages; but if they wanted to do so, printing should be simple (generally speaking, each page is printed in two or three parts). Browsers already have a "print" button or menu. It's not advisable to implement another additional button that generates PDF files the user can print later. This will make users waste time.

### 107 › Counters

What's the use of writing: "You are user 19,380" or "7,053,968"? Users are unique and they don't want to be seen as a number. They won't pay more or less attention to you just by knowing how many users have accessed your Website. They will become loyal if you treat them right and if they find what they want.

### 108 › It's your Website, not of the sponsors

Whenever you sell an ad, remember that you sell because users want to visit your Website. Never cover your content with external advertising. By doing this you will only drive users away. Consequently, you will lose sponsors.

### 109 › Inefficient or inexistent internal search engine

The search engine is one of the most important items on a Website. This is why there is nothing more frustrating than having a search engine that doesn't search, or an inexistent one, especially when it comes to working with a very large Website and with data bases. Users should be able to find what they want without any difficulties.

### 110 › Easy to Find with a Search Engine

If your Website has a search engine—something highly advisable—it's important that it be easy to find. The most advisable thing is to use conventions and standards, since users are generally used to finding them at the top right part of the Website.

# TIME IS MONEY

"Sometimes when you innovate, you make mistakes. It is best to admit them quickly, and get on with improving your other innovations."

**Steve Jobs**
**Co-founder of Apple Inc. and Pixar Animation Studios.**

# DON'T MAKE ME THINK, OR WASTE MY TIME

## 111 › You are here

Make sure users always know what their location is in the Website. This may seem obvious, but it isn't. Indicate users where they are. Write with links, through menus so that they know where they were and how they got there (e.g.: products -> design -> Web).

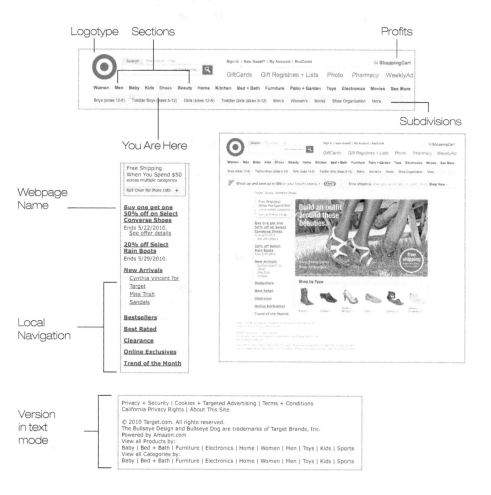

Image: Target.com

**112** › **Don't use an initial webpage with just a logo and a link to the Website**

When users access a webpage they don't want to waste time. They need to know what it's about and a logo with a "click here" message says nothing. It only invites them to leave the Website.

**113** › **Don't disturb or confuse users with the type of release**

If you need to ask users what Flash release, bandwidth or browser they have, they will most likely not know the answer. It has been proven that 95 per cent of the time users don't know. And if they can only access the information by providing this answer, it is highly probable that they will leave the Website before they can even enter.

**114** › **Use a simple navigation structure**

Don't confuse users. The simpler and more intuitive is the use of menus, the easier it'll be for them to go wherever they want.

**115** › **Include access to the main webpages at the footer of each page**

When the Website has many menus and submenus, it's advisable to use— no matter how redundant it may seem—access back to the main webpages, so that users can quickly go where they need to.

**116** › **Develop a webpage based on the user's need, not yours**

If you're the only one who understands the webpage, what's the point? Users are used to standards. Use conventions: don't change the name of a button for another of your invention because users won't understand what they are supposed to do.

**117** › **If you have to explain how to navigate the Website, redesign it!**

Unless it's a game, or an advanced system, links have to be descriptive enough for users to click on "click here" if they are interested in the topic. If you need to place "click here" all over the place, then the Website is probably poorly built.

## 118 › **New content difficult to find**

If the Website is updated on a permanent basis, it's a must to tell the frequent user where the new information is, in a clear and accurate way. Users come back because they think the Website will give them more of what it's given before; they will seldom come back to see what they've already seen.

## 119 › **Avoid using very long webpages**

Lean on the potential of the Web. This medium is not like a printed book. Take advantage of the possibility of using links to break down the information into multiple pages and offer users the chance to go to the contents they really need. (See Tip 33)

## 120 › **Be consistent in the resources you use**

If you use one language, respect it. Don't mix visual or usability languages, since they will only confuse users and it will look unprofessional. (See Tip 128)

## 121 › **Avoid a Page that is permanently too wide**

Even if ideally, users should never have to use the vertical scroll bar, when this happens they understand it and accept it. But bear in mind that users are not used to using the horizontal scroll bar.

This is why it is convenient to know what the current screen standards are, so that the Website doesn't exceed the standard width (currently 1024 x 768 pixels). Another option is to program the screen so that it automatically adapts to the page width of the user (although this is complex and you must evaluate whether investing in the technological development is worth it).

Favicon.ico

Image: PAHEF.org

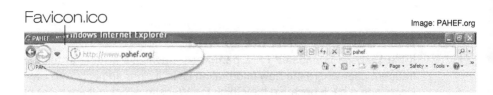

## 122 › Add to favorites

Give users an easy stay. If users think that your Website is important and worth adding to their favorites, offer the possibility of adding your webpage through a button on the menu. Don't forget to place the Favicon* icon (favicon.ico) on the browser bar. Also give users the possibility of saving the bookmark in Delicious**, or provide the "Like" button for their Facebook profile.

## 123 › Navigation menu difficult to find and use

The menu should stand out as such. If we develop a Website where the menu is camouflaged within the Website, it's pointless because users don't understand it. Content needs to be accessed in a simple way.

## 124 › Surprise without confusing

The interface has to be like a classic and efficient butler: a gentle and subtle guide, but never an annoying presence.

\* Favicon (short of Favorites Icon) is the Website's bookmark icon. Favicons are viewed by most browsers. It's a small 16 x 16 pixel square that is installed in the Website's root directory. See Tip 122 image.

\*\*Delicious *(www.delicious.com)* is a social network specialized in bookmarks that allows its users to save, share and discover links to Websites.

### 125 › Links of visited webpages must change their color

Users want to know if they have already visited a certain page so that they don't waste time reading the same thing again. Therefore, it's essential to respect the standards of active and visited links.

### 126 › Differentiate a Website from printed material

A printed leaflet is read in a linear way, starting always from the first or the last page (depending on the language on which it was written). But Websites are totally different: users can access a Website from any point on the Page and not from only a particular one. (See Tip 7)

### 127 › Use your printed material

If you already have brochures and printed material, you can use it in your Website in Flash, ebook or PDF format, so that users can "leaf through" the brochure or download it. Bear in mind that this material only adds information and doesn't compete with your Website.

### 128 › Usability and Functionality

These are key concepts for user retention. The simpler the Website is to navigate, the better built it is. Above all, if it works according to the expectations. The user experience will be better. Therefore, user permanence and return will be greater.

### 129 › Use auto-fill in text fields

When a user begins writing something standard into a text field, it's important to use the auto-fill function. This will help users quickly select what they are interested in and, above all, not make any mistakes when typing.

### 130 › Reduce the amount of clicks to the minimum

The user has to reach the information in no more than two or three clicks. Therefore, there is no need for many levels/sublevels. The simpler the navigation is, the better the user experience.

"

"What makes eBay successful...
the real value and the real power
at eBay is the community. It's the buyers
and sellers coming together and
forming a marketplace."

**Pierre Omidyar**
eBay founder

**131** › **RSS** (Really Simple Syndication)
If your Website is updated on a frequent basis, give users the possibility of subscribing to RSS. This is a format that enables sending Website subscribers new information whenever the Website is updated, without forcing users to revisit the Website searching for updates. To replicate the information special software is used. Additionally, you can resort to the RSS that comes with the last releases of browsers. (See Myths about SEO)

## 132 › Offer alternate means of payment
Even if the common denominator is to pay with credit cards, offer to pay through other means, if possible: cash on delivery, checks, money orders, etc. Furthermore, if you use credit cards, aside from the *Merchant Account* that you choose, offer the possibility of using PayPal®, as a great many users already have an existing verified account.

## 133 › Accept international transactions
By being on the Internet your business stops being local and becomes global. Accept credit card transactions from other countries. Verify if you have to pay for any charges and/or if you are authorized to export your product or service. Also keep in mind the shipping and customs costs, the travel time, etc. if you can generate commercial transactions with other countries. Add a currency converter to your Website.

## 134 › Offer shipping options
If your Website sells products that need to be delivered to the client, the shipping cost will have an impact on the final value your client will pay. Offer options so that clients can control the final price of the product, according to their needs.

## 135 › Listen to your client
If the user is kind enough to make a suggestion or observation about your Website, don't disregard it. Thank this person, since most users will leave your Website and not come back without giving you any kind of explanation. (See Tip 92)

# 4: REPUTATION

## (OR WHAT THEY'RE SAYING ABOUT YOU)

Look after your Website's reputation
with the same dedication you put
into your company, your brand or
even yourself. A good reputation
is the basis of good business.
This is especially true online.

# ONLINE REPUTATION

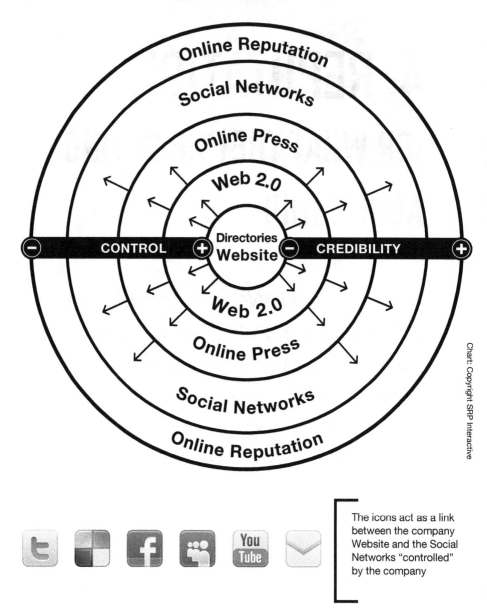

Chart: Copyright SRP Interactive

The icons act as a link between the company Website and the Social Networks "controlled" by the company

The chart shows that apart from having an excellent Website, the important thing is to have a good Online Reputation. The organization's Website is placed at the center of the chart and towards the edges the entire Web that builds the online reputation. If we make an analogy with the real world, it's like the difference between advertising and public relations. The company Website has more control over the messages, but less credibility, since it's what the company says about itself (just like in advertising). On the contrary, as we get closer to the external circles, the credibility is greater (just like with Public Relations campaigns), since it's what others say about the company.

Social Networks work as a link between both worlds.

# CREDIBILITY

**136** › **Monitor your online reputation\* (ORM)**

Users are increasingly "googling" your company name, your brand and even your executives, looking for information or simply trying to access your Site. The results of that search generate an amount of information that gets to the user through different sources through the Web, all of which finally build your online reputation.

As it happens offline, what another person says about you is always more credible than what you say about yourself.

In the chart on page 82 we can clearly see that as we get closer to the center, that is to say, to the corporative Website, there is more control over the messages but less credibility. As we move farther from the circle, credibility increases, but control over the messages decreases.

Monitoring online reputation is important in order to neutralize negative messages, and highlight positive ones that appear on Blogs, Websites 2.0, Social Networks, newspapers and the ever-growing number of Sites that keep growing on a daily basis. Pay special attention to Facebook.\*\*

\* Online Reputation Management, or ORM is the continuous research and analysis of the personal or professional reputation of a business or an industry, represented by online media content. It is also known as Online Reputation Monitoring.

\*\* The Social Network Facebook had a higher number of hits than Google in the United States, according to Experian Hitwise, a company that measures Internet traffic. In all, Facebook accumulated 7.07 % of the hits of American Internet users, compared to 7.03% of the giant search engine. The study confirms the unstoppable increase of the Facebook audience, whose visits have increased by 185% last year in the U.S., compared to Google's 9%. In fact, the Social Network has already had a higher number of hits than this search engine on certain festivities, such as Christmas and Christmas Eve. Experian Hitwise carries out its measurements on a base of 10 million American households and one million Websites in 160 countries. The spectacular increase of Facebook's traffic indicates the growing evolution of the Internet towards Social Networks and open networks, where users can upload their contents. In that sense, Google has been slow to react: its Social Network Orkut has scarce impact outside some specific markets such as Brazil, and it was only last month that Google launched Buzz, a similar system partly related to Gmail, their online e-mail, which has been subject of strong controversy due to its privacy problems. Source: Information published by the newspaper El Mundo (Spain).

### 137 › **Sometimes unbranded is better**

With the same criteria, many companies intelligently design unbranded Websites, generally using the slogan of one company or some other strategy with the purpose of making the message less corporate looking. Some intelligent examples that are worth looking at:

*www.eatbetteramerica.com* sponsored by General Mills.

*www.willyoujoinus.com* sponsored by Chevron.

*www.saludfemenina.com.ar* sponsored by Laboratorio Elea.

### 138 › **Safe Sites**

Users are naturally scared of leaving their credit card information on a Website. For this reason, if you don't have the corresponding security standards, the best thing is not to ask for the credit card number or personal data. The simplest solution is to put a telephone contact and to have all the transactions done through this means. There is nothing worse than undermining users' trust, who after having entered their credit card on your Website, become victims of fraud.

### 139 › **Be honest**

Don't promise on what you can't deliver systematically.

## 140 › Languages III

If you're going to develop your Website in a language that is not your mother tongue, have it translated by professionals in the area, and make sure to have qualified staff answer questions in the language of the user. It doesn't make sense to have a poorly translated Website or having one in a language nobody in the company can handle. Above all, never use software to translate without the intervention of human beings.

## 141 › Testimonials

Harvest your good reputation on the Web by stimulating feedback from your clients. If you carry out Corporate Social Responsibility (CSR) activities mention them on your Website.

## 142 › Copyright I

Make sure that everything you put on your Website abides by the Copyright laws, and that you have the right to use the material. Images, sound, music, videos, software, texts, advertising models, games, applications, unless they weren't developed by you, must be copyrighted. If your company is the one producing them, make sure you are complying with all the details in writing.

## 143 › Copyright II

Copyrights have a due date, since they are contributions for humanity as a whole. But the fact that a certain song does not pay copyright doesn't mean that you are entitled to buy a CD and uploading its music to the Website.
Music has:
- Musical composition (Copyright of the author for lyrics and music)
- Execution (Copyright of the performer)
- Phonogram (Copyright of the person recording and commercializing the music)

Just as an example, if you want to use classical music performed by Zubin Metha and recorded by Sony, ask for the copyright owners for an estimate before putting your idea in practice, because if you don't, you will be breaching the Copyright law.

"It takes 20 years to build a reputation and five minutes to ruin it. If you think about that, you'll do things differently."

**Warren Buffett**

CEO of Berkshire Hathaway

Image: YouTube.com

# READABILITY AND DESIGN
## (OR HOW TO LOOK PROFESSIONAL)

### 144 › Readability is above design

Make sure users can read what you write. Using very sophisticated fonts (typography) can go against users.

Whenever a font is chosen, you have to bear in mind that users will only see it in the same way if they have the same font installed in their computer. This is why it is essential to use fonts that come with the operating system and that are standards for users. Examples: Verdana, Arial, Georgia, Times New Roman. If you want to use special fonts, then you should use images, but you should bear in mind that they won't be good for search engines, since they don't read the content of images.

### 145 › Typography

Just like in any design project, Typography plays an essential role to adequately convey your ideas.
- Choose the Typography well
- Make sure it is readable and has the necessary size
- Don't use too many different Typographies (except when it's an online catalog to sell Typography)

### 146 › Use typography measurements carefully

In most cases, designers use Typography measurements (fonts) in points other than in specific terms (em*). Remember that the point or pt measurements are used for design on paper, whereas the "em" is the best option to use on the Internet. (See Tip 83)

---

* Em: Unit of typographic measurement used often in digital media because of its scalable value that allows users to define the typography size with which they want to visualize the texts.

## 147 › Lorem Ipsum

This Latin term is the name commonly used to show Typographies or design drafts to demonstrate what they will look like before inserting the final text.

Before launching your Website, make sure to eliminate all the filler text (FPO, For Placement Only). There is nothing more unpleasant than finding filler text just to fill space in a Website. This will make you look unprofessional and it will give the idea that you haven't had time to look at your own Website. If you didn't have the time, why would somebody else?

## 148 › Design your webpage bearing in mind smartphones

To view the webpage on smartphones, everything related to JavaScript and Flash has to be avoided. If you wish to use these technologies in your webpage, make two versions: one for desktop users and another one for phone users. (See Tips 54 and 60)

The image on the right shows a Freshdirect truck, belonging to a leading online supermarket from New York City, with an ad about a new system that allows users to shop in their Website using the iPhone.

Image: FreshDirect, LLC. FreshDirect is a registered Trademark of FreshDirect, LLC; iPhone is a registered Trademark of Apple, INC.

### 149 › Be careful with drop down menus

If you don't design a well developed drop down menu, it's likely that it won't be viewed by all browsers, nor by mobile phones, especially by smartphones.

### 150 › Make links visible

Users need to quickly recognize what a link is and where it leads to.

### 151 › Don't underline or color normal text unless necessary

The user may confuse it with a link and think that the Website doesn't work properly.

### 152 › Don't use strong colors

They can end up having poor visibility for users, as well as giving them a headache and making the page illegible.

### 153 › Avoid shifting text

When you have a link embedded in a block of text, make sure that on mouseover, there isn't a change in the font size, or that the text becomes bold, as this will inevitably move the text and disrupt reading.

### 154 › Don't fill the Website with messages (Badges)

The information that we want to provide should be on the page concerned. If it's necessary to communicate something special, we should only put that on the first page. But we shouldn't try to communicate everything at the same time. A Website packed with information loses effectiveness and looks very unprofessional.

### 155 › Don't mix advertising with content

If you want to advertise on your site, designate a space to do it. Don't mix it with your contents. The user can be misled and believe that it's part of the Website, and as a result, become disappointed and angry.

(See Tip 109)

### 156 › Beware of spelling and grammar mistakes

All the effort you put into designing and putting content on your page may be futile if the user perceives it as unprofessional due to these types of errors.

### 157 › Leave blank space

It's impossible to read something if you don't leave white space. Without it, users cannot perceive the level of importance of different elements.

### 158 › Specify the background color

If you don't specify the background color, you run an unnecessary risk.. If, for example, you want the background to be white and the visitor to the Website has the background on the browser configured to gray, then your Website will look unprofessional and have poor visibility.

### 159 › Don't make a text-only Website

While it's true that we must design taking speed, compatibility between browsers or smartphones, among other variables, into consideration, it's important to provide the user with an inviting Website. That's why you should always include some sort of image that will make the Website friendlier.

### 160 › Be available!

Always pick up your phone, reply to e-mail or chat messaging (during your established office hours). Help users to get in touch with you. If your company offers toll free 1–800 numbers or Skype, as well as the possibility of chatting, then you'll be one step ahead of the game.

### 161 › Add a Skype or Google Voice button

Provide users with easy ways to connect to you. Help them avoid having to call you. These two tools allow them to either talk or chat with you at a very low cost.

### 162 › Place banner ads on top or to the right

Users expect to see them there. It's important that advertising does not interfere with the content. (See example on the next page)

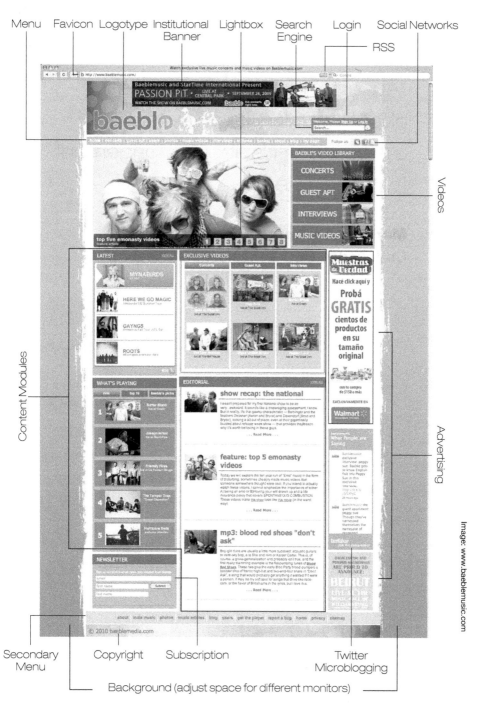

Menu · Favicon · Logotype · Institutional Banner · Lightbox · Search Engine · Login · Social Networks · RSS · Videos · Content Modules · Advertising · Secondary Menu · Copyright · Subscription · Twitter Microblogging · Background (adjust space for different monitors)

We love this Home Page because it's well-organized. All information, including advertising is variable so it is particularly important that the user can understand what it is at a glance.

"

"Advertising on the Web is less
about just hitting someone with
a message... It's about engagement
[with that user]."

**Mark Zuckerberg**
Co-founder, CEO & President of Facebook

### 163 › Know the limits of the WYSIWYG* editor

When you copy from a text editor such as Word to a WYSIWYG Editor, a lot of extra code is generated which when displayed on the webpage, can generate errors and therefore not be displayed correctly.

### 164 › Generate realistic images

Although it's not necessary for 3D images to look hyper-realistic, it's essential for them to look realistic enough to take users on a ride through their own imagination. If the 3D has anything to do with your business, it's essential for you to have a thorough understanding of Second Life** *(www.secondlife.com)* and how the user interacts with it. Note that Second Life offers visitors the chance to interact with virtual spaces.

### 165 › Surprise Factor

Look for the opportunity to create something unexpected.

* WYSIWYG (What You See Is What You Get) refers to HTML editors with a menu similar to Word. What you see when you write something is the same as displayed when shown through HTML.

** Second Life is a 3D virtual world created by Linden Lab and distributed in a wide network of servers that can be used via the Internet. This program provides to its users or 'residents' tools to modify the world and participate in its virtual economy that operates like a real market.

"Technology is always evolving, and companies—not just search companies—can't be afraid to take advantage of change."

**Eric Schmidt**
CEO of Google

# 5: TECHNOLOGY
## (OR GET TO KNOW YOUR BEST FRIEND)

To be in charge of a Website or an online business, it's not necessary for you to be a technology expert. But you should know that the better you understand it and the more open your mind is to incorporating new technologies, the easier it'll be for you.*

* Not understanding technology while having an e-commerce Website could be compared to having a store at a mall that you have never visited. How could you possibly know what to sell there without knowing what kind of people shop nor how they behave there? There are no shortcuts: to understand digital technology, you must interact with it.

# CORE LIBRARY

## LIB_NETWORK.H

```
struct Network{
  User_Library ulib;
  File_Library flib;
  Delay_Unit dunit;
}

Methods:
allocate_network();
initialize_network();
```

## CORE LIBRARY

## LIB_FILE.H

```
struct Owner_Node{
  int owner;
  int is_valid;
  Owner_Node* next;
}

struct File{
  int num_owners;
  Owner_Node* head_node;
  Owner_Node* tail_node;
}
```

## LIB_USER.H

```
enum user_t{
  good,
  mal_pure,
  mal_feed,
  mal_prov,
  mal_disg,
  mal_sybl,
  unknown
}

struct User{
  user_t behav
  int num_files
  float pct_clea
  float pct_hon
  BWidth_Unit
  Relation[NUM
}

struct User_Lib
  User* users
```

## LIB_DELAY.H

```
struct Trans{
  int commit_cycle;
  int send;
  int recv;
  int file_num;
  int valid;
}
```

```
struct Delay_Unit{
  Trans[BAND_PER]t_queue
}
```

```
struct File_Library{
  File[NUM_FILES] files.
}
```

# UNDERSTANDING TECHNOLOGY

### 166 › Always evolve
Nothing is forever. The only constant thing is change. If your Website works well today, it's not a sure thing that it will work well with tomorrow's technology. Try using the Site from all browsers for computers as well as from smartphones. (See Tip 183)

### 167 › Create a test environment (Beta)
Try to have a testing environment to test your Website in its entirety, especially if it has programming.

### 168 › Beware when testing
Conducting tests based solely on Internet Explorer and then putting the Site on the Web can lead to many headaches. Internet Explorer misses coding errors and displays the page without problems, but other browsers will not.

### 169 › W3C*
Familiarize yourself with the W3C standards. They will help you look good on all browsers. Test every page of your Website on *http://jigsaw. w3.org/css-validator*.

### 170 › Don't use blinking text
Not all browsers support it. Plus, it's not a W3C standard.

### 171 › Invalid HTML attributes
As mentioned, it's recommended that you follow the standards. On some browsers, certain functionalities might give you errors. Use CSS ** instead of specifications within the HTML. For <script> elements use "type" and not "language" to specify the language (usually JavaScript).

* World Wide Web Consortium (W3C) is an international consortium whereby member organizations and the general public work together to develop Web standards. Its mission is to lead the Web towards its full potential by developing protocols and guidelines that ensure the future growth of the Web.

** CSS (Cascading Style Sheets) is a file that acts as a template which defines the different styles of the elements of the Website.

**172 › Error in the DOCTYPE declaration**
It's the first statement that appears in the HTML. It helps browsers determine which version of HTML is used by each site, giving an indication as to which syntax and grammar are being used.

**173 › Nonexistent DTD (Document Type Definition)**
Here you define the types of elements and attributes that can be used on the page. It is written in the DOCTYPE tag.

**174 › Content-type contrary to server**
Sometimes the server sends a certain content type and the Website specifies another one to your site. This confuses the user's browser and special characters are not readable. This especially occurs with letters outside of the English language alphabet, accents and quotation marks. Be especially careful with these details.

**175 › Don't comment HTML on the page**
Only do so if it helps to comment the coding, but not to eliminate lines of code. Doing so makes the page unreadable for maintenance and increases the file size of the pages needlessly.

**176 › Encode pages in a particular language**
This helps search engines when it comes to indexing Websites, saying that the page is full of words in a determined language, although words in other languages can also be found.

**177 › JavaScript within the HTML body**
As with CSS, JavaScript has to be used from within the HTML calling for an external file. The advantage here is that JavaScript is downloaded, cached and reused the next time that it is required.

**178 › Don't use HTML to create the aesthetics of webpages**
If you have to define the layout (design) and the aesthetics of the page, do so through CSS. HTML only helps to build content.

## 179 › Use style sheets embedded in documents (css)

When developing a Website, a minimal expectation is for there to be consistency across every page. That's why if you define a style, it's recommended that you create it in an auxiliary file and call that file from every other HTML page, rather than insert it into every page as lines of code. If there is an external style file called from all other pages, it makes it easier when you want to change something about them (e.g. the font). So it's only necessary to change a single style file instead of changing all pages of the Site.

## 180 › When using CSS you must specify units

In CSS the width and height values must always be specified, unless they are 0. In contrast, in HTML it's not necessary, because it assumes the standard.

## 181 › Update the Page Code and replace it with CSS

Many pages were developed long ago and were never updated. Updating them will not only allow them to work better, but make them friendlier to search engines and browsers used by visitors.

## 182 › Don't use a browser specific CSS

Take into account that there are codes that only work on one browser. (E.g. scroll bar style, filters, etc.).

## 183 › Compatibility between browsers

Make sure your Website is compatible with all available browsers. No two browsers work exactly the same way, or interpret CSS and JavaScript in the same way. That is why it is extremely necessary to review the compatibility between the Website and the different Web Browsers (Internet Explorer, Safari, Firefox, Chrome, among others).

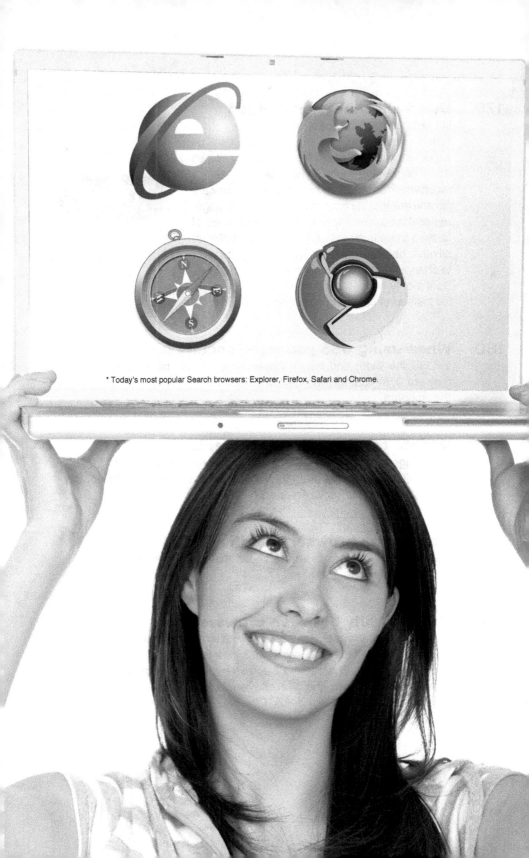

* Today's most popular Search browsers: Explorer, Firefox, Safari and Chrome.

**184** › **Don't try to get your Website to detect the browser and send specific code to it.**
This approach adds unnecessary complexity and whenever there is a new browser—or a new release of it—it stops working. It's easier and cheaper to test and make your Website work on all search engines, than to develop something like this.

**185** › **Class Nomenclature or ID**
When defining the name of any ID, it's not advisable to use a name referring its current appearance. For example, if you place a red dividing bar and call it "redbar"; then, you would have to change the name to "purplebar" throughout the Website, if you later changed the color to purple. Unfortunately, most of the time, only the color is changed, but not the original nomenclature which leads to confusion.

**186** › **Invalid class or ID names**
It's important to ensure that the IDs specified within HTML are defined within the corresponding CSS, as this can lead to the page not appearing correctly.

**187** › **Develop a CMS** (Content Manager System)
If you use databases, develop a content management system to help you update pages via templates without the need for a Web designer.

**188** › **Use technology to fit the user**
Keep in mind this idea: the more novice the user is the simple and clearer the interface of the Website should be.

**189** › **Useless Meta Elements**
There is a tendency to use many Meta Tags, but it is important to take into account that many of them are not processed by search engines and others only serve to promote the author of the page. Therefore, it's preferable to place greater emphasis on the content of the Website that in completing the Meta Tags* page.

---

* Meta Tags are HTML characters that tell search engines the words to find the page that contains them.

## 190 › Use the correct image format

The basic formats for use on the Internet are JPEG, GIF and PNG. Consider the qualities of each format and use them intelligently:

- **JPEG** is excellent for displaying millions of colors and shades, since it shows color in 24 bits. The cons are that for the file size to be small, quality is lost and it cannot be used with transparency.
- **GIF** only reproduces colors in 8 bits (256 colors in total). It's good for maps and color images with transparency, as well as for moving images, "Animated GIFs" (layers of overlapping images).
- **PNG** is used in photos and graphics, and allows transparency. They are better than GIF, but of lesser quality than JPEG.

Always test the size-quality relation of the image.

## 191 › Everything counts: Hosting too

Many customers choose to host their Website in the United States in order to benefit from the quality and speed of service Providers (ISP *) and network connections. However, if your objectives are local, please note that, for example, Google Brazil prioritizes search through a Site whose IP belongs to that country. Of course there are other technical considerations to take into account, but if your goal is local, don't forget this detail. Always test the response time of the hosting.

## 192 › Be careful when "refreshing" DNS

When you change IP** or server, you must take into account that for all Internet servers on a global scale to become informed, it may take up to 36 hours. It's necessary, therefore, to have the old and the new Website active during this time. The biggest problem arises when sales are made or the Web is transactional, as changes may be lost or generate losses.

## 193 › Special uncoded characters

If you have to show special characters such as accents, &, letters that are not from the English language, white space, etc., it is necessary to convert them to a set of special characters (HTML entities) and define the specific coding Meta Tag "charset".

---

* ISP Internet Service Provider

** IP is a unique number expressed in the format xxx.xxx.xxx.xxx that is used to identify a Website or a computer.

## 194 › Generate Sitemap, URLlist, Robots.txt

These files are very important for search engines. They report which pages and which pages not to index. The Sitemap is used by "crawlers" (programs that inspect webpages) to find the content of a Website. Many CMS applications (Content Management Systems) can generate a Sitemap automatically. (See Tip 187)

## 195 › Use AJAX wisely

Like JavaScript, you shouldn't overuse AJAX *. Its main use is to change information on the page without uploading it again.

## 196 › HTML vs. Flash

If despite everything, you still want to build 100% Flash Website, you should expect higher development costs than if you did it entirely in HTML. Also expect less visibility, because as we said before, Flash is invisible to search engines. Please be aware that building your Website in Flash will keep you from getting statistics (unless you develop your own set of statistics) and you will not know what happens within the Website. (See Tip 67)

---

* AJAX (Asynchronous JavaScript and XML) is a technique used to create interactive applications or RIA (Rich Internet Applications). With these applications, you can make changes on webpages without having to upload them again.

## 197 › Beware of the browser's cache*

Changes are often made on a Website, but because the user or the company have "cached" information, the changes cannot be seen, unless you delete the cache or press <CTRL><F5> at the same time.

## 198 › Portability

If for some reason you change Internet Hosting service provider, you shouldn't assume the page will work without making changes to it, especially if it's developed in PHP or ASP, or if it has defined forms. Often, the software versions of servers make it necessary to add or modify something.

## 199 › User Login

If you put a section of login and password, make sure it is protected. Use security mechanisms through SSL Security certificates (Secure Socket Layer Key )**. (See Tip 138)

## 200 › Password protection

Users rarely use a different password for each access. They usually have a set of passwords to enter the different Sites they use. That's why when you send information through the Internet make sure that the password is encrypted.

* Cache: the browser used by an individual and / or proxy server in a corporate network temporarily save webpages in their memory to reduce traffic and provide faster display of Pages that have been previously visited.

**SSL: a security protocol that has the distinct feature of displaying the image of a padlock on the browser when a user enters a Site. This tells visitors that the information exchanged in these webpages will not be intercepted by anyone.

# EXTENSIONS MOST USED ON THE INTERNET

| EXTENSION | ▶ CONFIGURATION |
| --- | --- |
| **ASA** | Contains statements of objects, variables and methods that are accessed by all ASP pages of the application |
| **HTACCESS** | Apache Configuration File |

| EXTENSION | ▶ GRAPHICS |
| --- | --- |
| **GIF** | Graphics Interchange Format (See Tip 190) |
| **ICO** | Icon (See Tips 99 and 122) |
| **JPG** | JPEG Image (See Tip 190) |
| **PNG** | PNG Image (See Tip 190) |

| EXTENSION | ▶ LANGUAGE EXECUTED IN THE USER'S COMPUTER |
| --- | --- |
| **AJAX** | Asynchronous JavaScript and XML (See Tip 195) |
| **CGI** | A generic protocol which can extend the capabilities of HTTP |
| **CSS** | CSS (See Tip 179) |
| **HTM** | Hypertext Markup Language - webpage |
| **HTML** | Hypertext Markup Language - webpage |
| **JS** | JavaScript (See Tip 131) |
| **RSS** | RSS (See Tip 131) |
| **XHTML** | Extensible Hypertext Markup Language |
| **XML** | Extensible Markup Language |

| EXTENSION | ▶ SERVER-SIDE LANGUAGE * |
| --- | --- |
| **ASP** | Active Server Page - Microsoft |
| **ASPX** | ASP.NET script page - Microsoft |
| **JSP** | JAVA |
| **PHP** | hypertext Preprocessor |

| EXTENSION | ▶ MOVIES |
| --- | --- |
| **SWF** | Movie developed in Flash (See Tip 67) |
| **SCR** | File in Microsoft Silverlight format (See Tip 95) |

| EXTENSION | ▶ SOUND |
| --- | --- |
| **MP3** | MPEG, audio layer 3 |
| **WAV** | Windows audio file format |

| EXTENSION | ▶ VIDEO |
| --- | --- |
| **FLV** | Flash Video |
| **F4V** | Flash Video in MPEG-4 format |
| **MOV** | QuickTime Video format |
| **MPG** | MPEG Video |
| **WMV** | Windows Media Video |

* Used to access databases.

"

"Think big and don't listen to people who tell you it can't be done. Life's too short to think small."

**Timothy Ferriss**
Author of the Bestseller "The 4-Hour Workweek"

Think small. Finding an unexplored niche can be very profitable...

# 6: PERFORMANCE

If you want your Website to be successful, read the statistics every day; understand what each parameter means, and change direction as many times as necessary.

# SEO WORK METHODOLOGY*

Chart: Copyright SRP Interactive

1 **Search:** Look for ranking, traffic, leadership, sales, competitors, online target, etc.
2 **Define Objectives:** : Identify measurable goals, focusing on the expectations and the ultimate goals you expect from your Site.
3 **Technical Analysis:** Conduct an SEO analysis of your current Site.
4 **Keyword Search:** Choose the best keywords to be known by the target audience.
5 **Content:** Develop content and text and insert the keywords with the adequate density based on your SEO.
6 **Promotions:** The development of links with well-established webpages is the best way to call the users' attention and to get better ranking on search engines.
7 **Subscription:** Register your Website to the best search engines and directories.
8 **Reports:** Generate a periodic report with the results and progress on your Website.

* SEO (Search Engine Optimization) is the result of information obtained from the databases of the major Internet search engines that use search algorithms in their software.

# MEASURE, MEASURE, MEASURE

## 201 › Listen to your statistics

*Google Analytics* is a very powerful software—and also free of charge—that will allow you to see what is going on in your Website from the user's point of view. Take advantage of it!

## 202 › Experiment the Website's usability

Try it from different computers (PC and Mac) with different hardware and software configurations, from different browsers. See if you can find it from Yahoo!, Google, Bing, etc. Ask people if they easily access the information.

## 203 › Test it all the time

Test your Website from different browsers, from different types of Web access (cable modem, ADSL, smartphones and even dial up) and with users of different ages and with diverse levels of experience.

## 204 › Review the objectives on a periodic basis

Your business is constantly changing and your Website must also reflect these changes. Technology evolves at a great speed... Do as much self-evaluation as you can: review the objectives and measure your performance.

## 205 › Change direction when necessary

If you see that your Website is being visited in pages you considered secondary and that you're not getting enough hits in the pages of your main business, first verify if the Website is well developed and crawlable; otherwise, change the focus of your business. Don't miss out on opportunities. Base yourself on statistics. (See Tip 206)

# TEST, TEST, TEST...

## 206 › Base yourself on statistics

Statistics are the key to understanding what is going on in your Website. Modify the HTML page in question and study the results until you find the desired point. Take advantage of the free of charge statistics system offered by ISPs (Internet Service Providers)—if you are not offered this feature it's a good reason to change Hosting. Read the statistics and make queries if there are details you don't understand. They will help you a lot to improve the performance and correct the direction.

Image: Google Analytics

# MAKE CORRECTIONS

**207** › **Correct to improve**

Reviewing, testing and staying up to speed with new technology are necessary, especially after having received suggestions or comments. The only missing thing to keep your Website or online business fully working is changing directions every time it's necessary. If a new browser or hardware is launched to the market, get access to them and test how your Website works from them. You will surely need changes there.

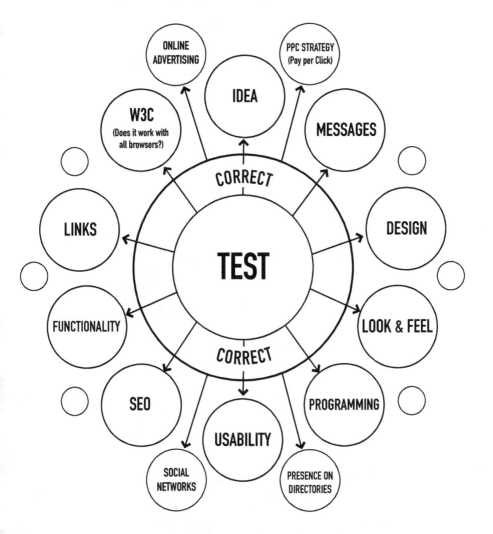

Chart: Copyright SRP Interactive

# 7: COMPETITORS

The Internet is a window to the world.
Just like you and your competitors are
observed by prospects, clients,
suppliers, future colleagues and
coworkers, you also have the chance
of doing the same in real time. Don't
miss out on this opportunity: a lot can be
learned by monitoring the market online.

(See chart on page 116)

"

## Threat or opportunity? *

The sensation of threat will always exist; this is why it's important to efficiently manage the online tools that give you a unique opportunity of measuring the competitors to get ahead of their moves.

**The key:** to integrate them in an efficient way to optimize time and above all to do it on a permanent basis.

* In a digital world, thinking that you don't have presence on the Internet because you simply don't have a Website or a Blog is an erroneous concept. With Social Networks, through a photo (Facebook, Flickr), a video (YouTube), Blog or network (LinkedIn) your company or yourself are referenced for better or for worse. Once this fact has been accepted as a reality, you have the power of being proactive to show how you want to be perceived.

# COMPETITORS

**208** › **Know your market**

Know how your competitors promote themselves, if they sell online or not, or if they only use the Internet for promotion or to give information. Know the world: explore, travel (even though it's on the Internet). Find unexploited niches that will help you make your business grow.

**209** › **Know your competitors well**

By being online, your competitors can end up being global. Don't ignore them if they are based in some other part of the world. Investigate, learn from them. They may end up being your strategic partners in the future.

**210** › **Make the price visible**

Take into account that users don't want to waste their time. They don't want to do all the purchase process of the product or service to find the price after having wasted precious time in your webpage. They want to know the price from the very beginning. Price is not the only purchase decision factor. It's important but not the only element. Don't hide it.

**211** › **Define your return policy**

A good return policy is an excellent sales engine because it encourages clients to buy without fear. Explain the policy before selling the service or product. Reinforce the message in the confirmation e-mail. A good example is the return policy of *www.zappos.com*\*: It's worth checking out.

**212** › **Fine tune your radar to look for competitors**

Just like you may be using your online presence to attack new global markets, your competitors (although you may be unaware of them) may be doing the same. Use the most frequent search engines—such as Google, Yahoo!, Bing or the Chinese one, Baidu—as a radar to know your competitors.

---

\* Zappos.com is an online footwear and apparel store. Since it was founded in 1999 in the United States, it has grown to be the largest shoe store of the world. The company was acquired by Amazon.com in 2007 for around 900 million dollars. Source: New York Times.

# 7 SIMPLE TOOLS
## TO MONITOR ONLINE COMPETITORS

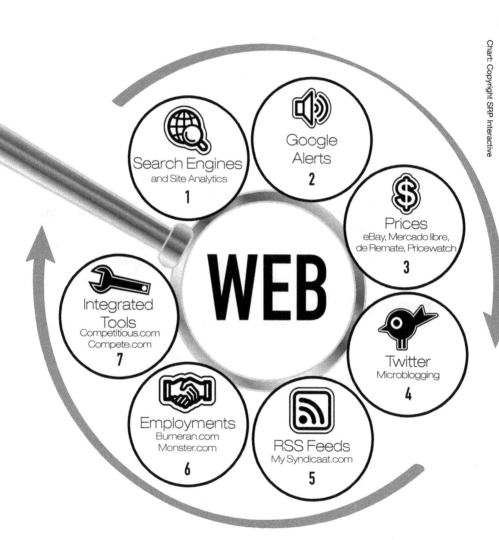

The chart shows seven simple tools that can be systematically used to monitor the activity of online competitors

# 8: POTENTIAL

Collaboration tools are increasingly becoming more important. They allow users to interact, share knowledge and cooperate in a dynamic environment regardless of distance, and companies to improve their productivity. While big companies develop their own "secret" and tailor-made* tools, small companies can use standard** online developments which allow them to be dynamic at an affordable cost.***

* With greater security levels and developed according to their specific needs and security policies.

** Explore *www.37signals.com*, a set of online collaboration software applications (Basecamp, Highrise, Backpack and Campfire) for small companies, which has more than 3 million users and is fully growing.

*** Conduct a proper analysis before hiring this type of service, since what at first may seem affordable, may end up being costly in terms of time and money after migrating data to another provider.

# COLLABORATION (WIKI)*

**213** › **A unique collaboration tool**

Probably one of the deepest changes caused by the Internet is the possibility of working in a network. The way professionals interact, make queries, collaborate, compare information, register, evaluate, teach and learn represents an unprecedented step forward for humanity.

A team of coworkers can work in a collaborative way, remotely and in a synchronized way, sharing online information but with restricted access for the rest of the users. Through the file robots.txt search engines can be instructed not to index your webpages online. (See Tip 194)

---

* The "Wiki" concept comes from a Hawaiian word that means "fast" and is used to name all the collaborative work Sites (E.g.: Wikipedia).

# EXPLORE THE WEB'S POTENTIAL

**214** › **The power of Social Networks (Social Media)**
Social Networks are an excellent option to keep close to your audience and to inform the latest news of your business, generating more traffic to your Website. Include your profile in the most suitable networks within your area of action and establish links from your Website. (See Tip 16)

**215** › **Nothing online is either free of charge or cheap any more**
There are still those who think that a Website has no development value because it belongs to the virtual world, or that even a Website may have no cost for the company and that it can work on its own, with no follow-up. Nothing could be further from the truth.

**216** › **Careful with the links that make you lose traffic**
Carefully evaluate the links you wish to have in your Website. A collection of links without a defined reason will make you lose traffic and hence, business.

**217** › **Make a Blog**
Blogs allow you to update information and generate traffic in your Website in a fast and simple way. Through the Blog you will be able to establish a valuable connection with your audience, offering useful information that will enrich the perception of users and encourage conversations. It's important that the Blog have quality content so that it is valued by the target audience. Pay the same attention you would pay to details on a printed publication.

### 218 › **Create a Forum**

This will give you the possibility of exchanging information among the community linked to your business, as well as increasing your contact base.

### 219 › **Recommend it to a friend**

The desired "word-of-mouth" effect has this format on the Internet. If users considered what you propose in your Website to be interesting enough, give them the option of recommending it to a friend. It is an excellent way of starting to generate virality*.

---

* Virality: The result of "Viral Marketing", term used to refer to marketing techniques that try to use the Social Networks and other electronic media to generate exponential increases in brand awareness through self-replicating viral processes analogous to the spread of computer viruses.

# EVOLUTION OF THE COMPANY'S ACTIVITY ON THE INTERNET

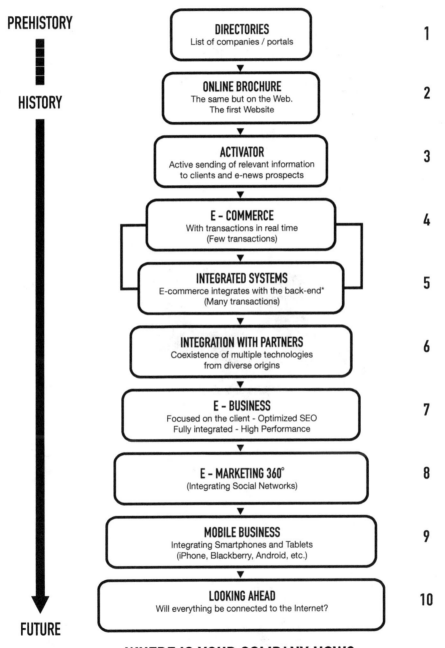

## WHERE IS YOUR COMPANY NOW?

* Front-end is the part of the software that interacts with users, whereas back-end is the part where data is uploaded to feed the front-end.

"The future depends on what we do in the present."

**Mahatma Gandhi**

# 9: FUTURE

There are many speculations about the future of the Internet and a few certainties. What is certain is that whoever is left out will miss out on opportunities. On the Internet, small companies challenge big corporations and in many cases they end up being the winners.*

The best way to know the future is by creating it.

* A clear example is the Mozilla Firefox browser, which has been able to capture more than 20% of the global market in less than 5 years, challenging Microsoft.

Does anyone remember Altavista?
Even if at the beginning of the Internet era Altavista was positioned as one of the most important browsers, it currently registers only around 61,000 searches per day, compared to the 200 million daily queries processed by Google. Altavista was created by Overture Service Inc., acquired by Yahoo!.

# FUTURE

> › Everything will be "connected to the Internet".
> › Terrorists of the future will attack the network.
> › Virtual reality will increasingly become more important.
> › Addiction to the network will be a global public health problem.
> › The network will be under more surveillance.*
> › Work will become more virtual.
> › There will be less privacy.
> › Whoever is not on the Internet won't have an identity.
> › There will be new ways of online payment.
> › There will be industries that will change forever.**

## 220 › Interaction with other users

Nowadays there are network games, like those offered on Facebook and the Wii console where you can send and receive information from and to other users; or games for Smartphones, where it's possible to send the information to compare score with others. In the future it will be possible to share whatever you want with whoever you want, segmenting it by topic. For example, you will be able to share information about what you have in your refrigerator with a support group to lose weight and members of this group could help you watch over the calories you consume. At the same time, this information could be shared with a supermarket and pre-establish that when the stock of a certain food reaches certain level, it gets automatically re-supplied. The possibilities are endless.

---

* Google disclosed details about the requests made by countries all over the world to deliver data about users or to censor information. With 291 requests from July to December 2009, Brazil was the country that urged Google the most to eliminate content. Germany was second, with 188 requests; India was the third, with 142, and the United States, fourth, with 123. These figures include the requests to remove material from YouTube, Google's video portal. Brazil also leads the list of identity requests, with 3,663; the United States comes second with 3,580 requests and the United Kingdom comes in a far third place, with 1,166 requests. Google stated that they cannot disclose the statistics about China's requests because they are considered to be secrets of State. In March 2010, Google withdrew its search engine from China due to problems related to online censorship. With this tool that breaks down figures on the Internet, the company hopes to take "only the first step towards a growing transparency". Information published on the BBC Site and by the newspaper El Mundo (Spain).

** As an example, we have already seen how, in less than one decade, the music industry changed forever and nowadays Apple through iTunes and the iPod are the ones who lead the global market of an industry that has changed in an unprecedented way. We have also seen how the stock image industry dramatically changed its business model (See Foreword by David Moffly).

# EVOLUTION OF THE MODEL

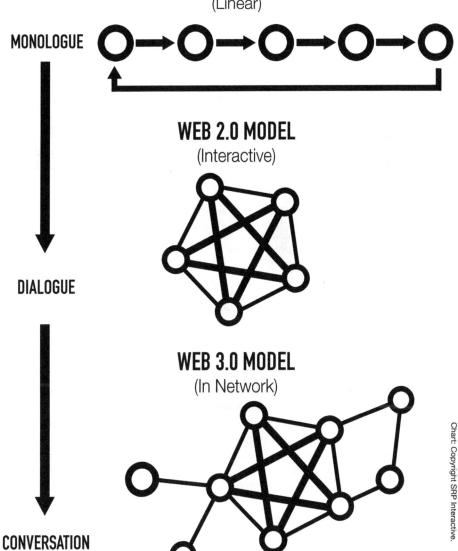

### WEB 1.0 MODEL
(Linear)

MONOLOGUE

### WEB 2.0 MODEL
(Interactive)

DIALOGUE

### WEB 3.0 MODEL
(In Network)

CONVERSATION

Chart: Copyright SRP Interactive.

Markets are conversations…

## 221 › **Connectivity**

In the future every electronic device will be connected to the Internet. Seeing how your Website is perceived through these devices will be an important part of the work to do, and according to your target audience, the results will be more important.

If you now have a Wii console, it can be connected to the Internet to navigate and/or enable new channels. If you work in the entertainment business you must pay a lot of attention to navigation through household consoles.

## 222 › **Never say never...**

Technologies change at an overwhelming pace and new generations relate to them in a different way from previous generations. So if you want to get to all the audiences, don't think that there is something you will never do. Open your mind and be willing to look at things under a new light.

"

In the near future people
will spend more time online
than watching TV*.

* A proof that accompanies this phenomenon is the way in which investment in online advertising is exponentially growing. While investment in advertising in air TV and cable TV is slowly growing and advertising in print media is decreasing. Source: IAB (Interactive Advertising Bureau) www.iab.net

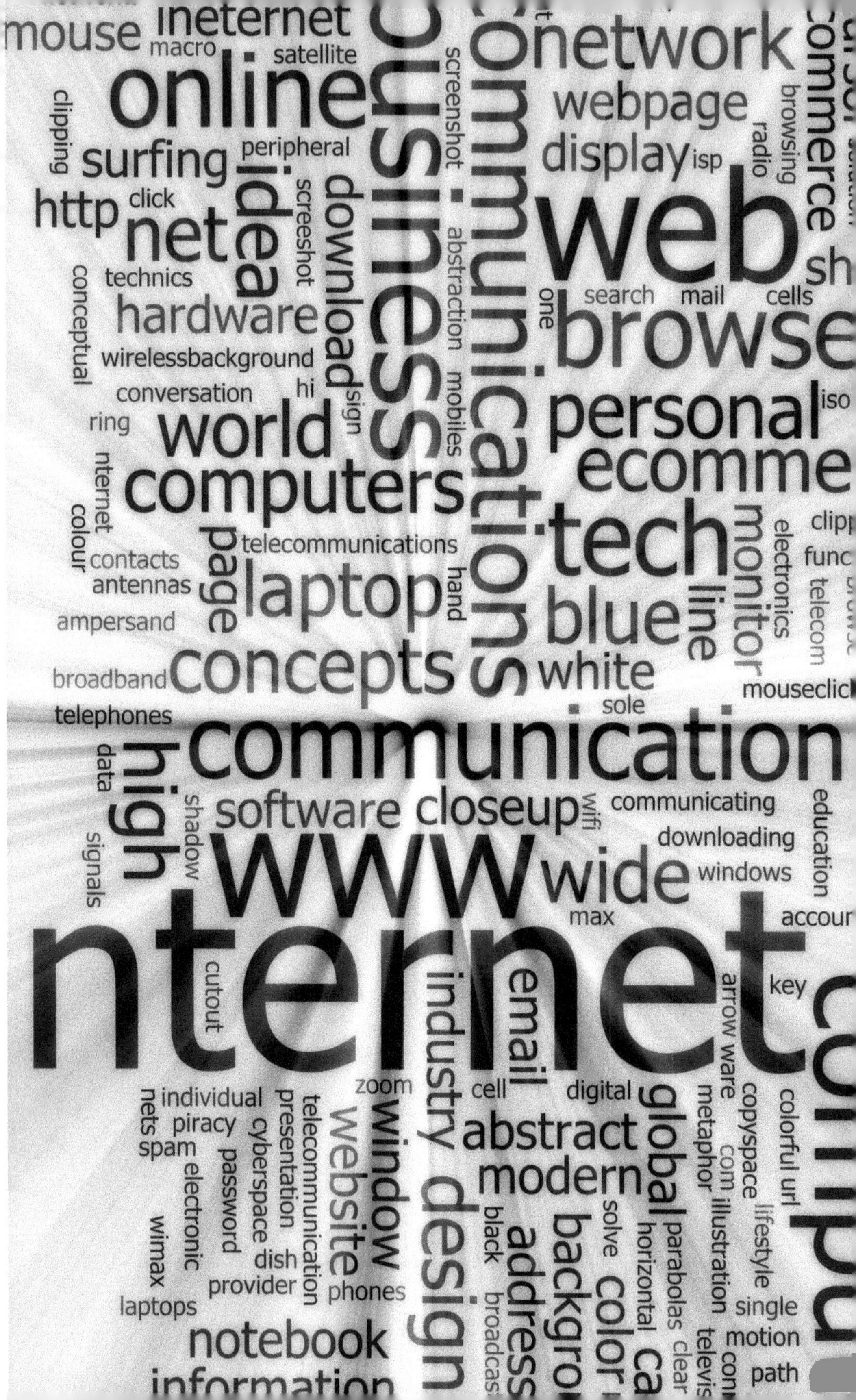
mouse
ineternet
macro
satellite
network
online
business
communications
webpage
display
isp
radio
browsing
commerce
clipping
surfing
peripheral
screenshot
http
click
net
idea
screeshot
download
web
technics
abstraction
search
mail
cells
conceptual
hardware
one
browse
wirelessbackground
conversation
hi
sign
mobiles
personal
iso
ring
world
ecomme
nternet
computers
colour
tech
monitor
electronics
telecommunications
contacts
antennas
page
laptop
hand
line
blue
telecom
ampersand
concepts
white
broadband
mouseclick
sole
telephones
communication
data
high
shadow
software
closeup
wifi
communicating
education
signals
downloading
www
wide
windows
max
nternet
cutout
industry
email
arrow
key
zoom
cell
digital
individual
nets
piracy
spam
cyberspace
presentation
telecommunication
website
window
abstract
global
metaphor
copyspace
com
colorful url
electronic
password
modern
wimax
dish
design
black
address
solve
background
horizontal
parabolas
illustration
lifestyle
provider
phones
color
laptops
single
notebook
broadcast
clear
motion
information
path

# 10: INTERNET MYTHS (A to Z)

From its beginnings, the Internet has been a medium full of myths and rumors that disseminate in a viral way because of its own nature. For instance, there are still people who still think: "the Internet is for porn..."*

* A recurrent statement of a character from the Broadway musical "Avenue Q" created in 2003, whose characters are puppets who sing about prejudices, racism, porn, drugs, homosexuality and even politics.

# IT'S EASY!

### A › I have a webpage, I have a company

During the dotcom boom many believed that this was possible. However, a Website is just a face of the company, maybe the most important one, but by no means can it hold as the company itself. (See Foreword by David Moffly)

### B › I have a webpage, I'm already making money

If that were the case, people with a Website would abandon their other work activities the same day they upload the Site to the Internet and they would live on whatever the Website generated. The Website is the first step, but the most important and difficult thing is to get traffic to the Website and to make it profitable.

### C › I'll upload the Site when it's perfect and then no longer change it

This could have been possible years ago, in the prehistory of the Web. Nowadays a successful Website is the consequence of daily work and of an interdisciplinary team of professionals who think about the user. Nothing is by chance.

# CONTENT

### D › If the webpage is done, I've already done most of the work

Honestly anyone can design a Website with a little dedication, but building a good Website requires a lot of work and professionalism. Once it is uploaded to the Internet, the second never-ending stage begins: getting traffic and turning users into clients.

### E › If the webpage doesn't look appealing it doesn't work

The most important thing about the Internet is being visible; if not, just analyze the cases of Craiglist, MySpace or eBay. These Websites don't stand out because of their aesthetics, and yet they work perfectly, thanks to the strategy and the proposed objectives. The key of these Websites is visibility, popularity and the benefits they offer.

**F ›** **If the webpage is not entertaining it doesn't work**

Whenever a Website is developed, it must be done thinking about the business objective and the target audience. If the end user has little time and wants to get in, do business and leave, an "entertaining" Site will distract him/her and this person will leave without doing business with you.

**G ›** **Content is not so important**

Users stay and come back to our Website if they consider the content they find to be important. If we don't offer anything interesting, why would they stay and return again later? (See chart on page 34)

# MARKETING

**H ›** **My business doesn't need to be on the Internet**

Although it seems incredible, we keep on hearing this statement. Probably many businesses can survive for a while if they are not on the Internet. But those who believe this myth should wonder about the possibilities they are missing due to the simple fact of not being on the Internet.

**I ›** **Doing marketing on the Internet is very expensive**

Throughout the book we have mentioned that it is essential to evaluate the cost-benefit ratio of the actions taken in different situations. It is true that money spent on online advertising and marketing can quickly disappear and with few obtained results. This is why it is necessary to continuously monitor the pace of actions. The Internet is not for lazy people.

# Search Engine Optimization*

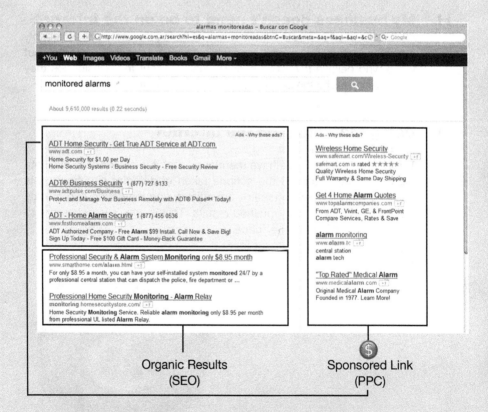

Organic Results
(SEO)

Sponsored Link
(PPC)

* SEO (Search Engine Optimization) is the result of the information obtained from the databases of the major Internet search engines that use search algorithms in their software.

# SEO (SEARCH ENGINE OPTIMIZATION)

**J** › **I do SEO and I forget about it**
Doing SEO (Search Engine Optimization) is an every day job. It's a never-ending race between your Website and those of your competitors. If you do nothing you will miss out on important opportunities.

**K** › **I do SEO and I'm N° 1 in Google, Yahoo! or Bing**
Don't trust someone who tells you this is possible. How are you going to appear before Google if you are offering a service offered by Google? Nobody can assure the results. On the other hand, don't forget that your competitors can always react and hire another SEO expert to position themselves above you.

**L** › **Google's algorithm is...**
A big mystery! Every Website developer and owner tries to guess its behavior to be able to better position their Websites, but there is nothing you can know with absolute certainty. Think that the algorithm of any search engine is like a living entity that evolves at the same speed of technology.

**M** › **The expert has assured success**
The user, either expert or ignorant, is the one who will finally decide the Website's failure or success. Don't ever forget that "the user is king". If you follow this book's indications, you will minimize the mistakes, but if you can't attract traffic and you don't generate certain empathy with the user, no expert will be able to help you.

# WEB ACCESSIBILITY

**N** › **Accessibility is only for disabled people**
Even if it's true that work is done so that any person with some kind of disability can enter and navigate the Internet, Web accessibility goes way beyond that: it's the ongoing search so that there are no limitations when it comes to having access to information.

O › **Web accessibility is building Websites that work regardless of the software or hardware used**

Web accessibility refers to respecting different people, their personal needs and likes. Not everyone uses the Web in the same way, or with the same type of equipment.

P › **Accessibility makes my Website look unappealing**

Whether a Website is very appealing or not has nothing to do with accessibility. Accessibility has to do with the way in which information is accessed, not with the way the Site looks. This concept does not refer to removing all the colors and images but to the way in which they are used.

Q › **Accessibility makes my Website economically non viable**

Like in every project, thinking before acting allows you to reduce costs dramatically. It's much less expensive to think of a Website from all the possible angles before starting to design it than having to change it or re-do it because users cannot access the information.

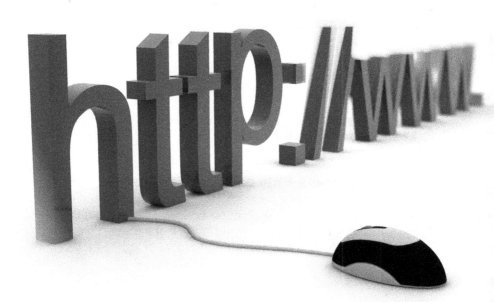

# SEARCH ENGINES

### R › ".org" Sites rank better

This is the opinion of many professionals. Many times ".org" domains rank better than other extensions such as "dotcoms". It depends on many factors, although the truth is only known to the corresponding search engine. (See Tip 15)

### S › If you have a good domain name, your Website will be well ranked

The statement "the domain name is everything" is relative. The popularity of a Website has to do with many more factors than that one. A good domain name helps, but it isn't everything. The evidence is clear.

# NAMES

### T › The domain name should only have existing words

While common words are easier to remember, search and position, nothing prevented Yahoo, YouTube or even Taringa!* to get to where they are today. You can register any name or word: the choice of domain name lies within your imagination and SEO and performance depend on the quality of the Website, the Blog and the frequency of updates.

### U › You can't use known brand names for new domain names

This statement is debatable. If you're not using the Site in a commercial way, taking advantage or affecting the brand in question, it's quite possible to use the name of this brand within your domain name. This is often the case when used for business purposes different to the actual brand. A common case is for Sites of law firms seeking clients who have been allegedly harmed by a brand or company. To make class action law suits, they use the brand in question within a phrase that makes up the domain name.

*Taringa! Taringa.net (collective intelligence) is a virtual community of Argentine origin frequently visited. Users here can share any type of content through a collaborative system of interaction.

http://search en

# SEARCH RESU

## 1. your we

"Google only has 3% of global advertising."

**Hal Varian**
Chief Economist at Google

# PAGERANK*

**V** › **The better the PageRank, the higher the traffic**
PageRank is independent of the number of visits

**W** › **PageRank depends on the quality of content**
This is not true: PageRank is determined by a mathematical formula, known only to Google, its creator.

**X** › **Having a high PageRank is essential in order to get good results in searches**
As mentioned earlier, PageRank is only one factor that improves the results partially. There are many variables that affect the positioning in Google.

**Y** › **PageRank is useless**
While PageRank shouldn't be the only thing that concerns you, it's good to pay attention to it since it is another indicator of whether you are doing things right on the Internet.

**Z** › **PageRank is lower in each sublevel**
If you compare the PageRank in each of the pages of your website, you will notice that every page ranks differently and that how it ranks doesn't necessarily decrease as the level of where the information is found goes deeper.

---

* According to Google, its creator, "PageRank performs an objective measurement of the relevance of webpages. To do so, it solves an equation that contains more than 500 million variables and 2 billion terms. In Instead of counting direct links, PageRank interprets a link from Page A to Page B as a vote for Page B from Page A. PageRank evaluates, thus, the importance of a given page based on the number of votes it receives."
Source: *www.google.com/intl/es/corporate/tech.html*

# OUR COMMITMENT TO THE COMMUNITY

We firmly believe that investing in education and encouraging the entrepreneurial spirit of people is the key to building a better world. 10% of the profits generated by the sale of this book will be donated to an NGO, with the goal of contributing to achieve this vision.

# FEEDBACK

As we suggest you to listen to your users, we would like to know your views on the Tips and the Myths published in this book. Likewise, we would like to count on your cooperation if you have new Tips you would like to share with us and other readers for the second edition.

You can contact us at: tips@srpinteractive.com or through the Website:

**www.222tips.biz →**

# AFTERWORD

By **Ana Rita Gonzalez**,
CEO of Policy Wisdom

Everything changes and everything stays the same, either you adapt or you fall behind. Life is a perennial Yin Yang. Before, waiting was the norm, with the frustration and excitement that anticipation brought with it. Today everything is instant, frustration has been replaced with the need to be connected ALL the time and emotion is now called "I'm already there".

When I started my career, the fax machine was the most sophisticated piece of technology. Today I have more battery chargers than cosmetics and I write text messages to those in the room next to me. My purse has to fit my laptop and everything I find on the Web, including recipes, purchases, the most complex research and even the love of my life.

The word "home" is not only the family household, but is now the virtual lobby for every webpage. "Wallpapers" are no longer on the walls and the "portal" is no longer a place I walk through. Even domains aren't what they used to be… and never has it been more common to have a privacy policy that today when we dare say everything on the Web.

My "social network" can be anywhere in the world but meets at my Facebook page. We may not be able to meet for coffee, but together we create a "virtual estate".

When somebody mentions "flash" no one assumes anymore that they're talking about photography, and besides the most common way to see pictures is digitally. A "mouse" is not a creature chased around by a cat, nor are "cookies" something you have with milk, and yet "pop-ups" have become better-known than popcorn.

The Web is part of our new way of life, with more positive attributes than challenges posed. It's a unique tool that allows me to see my loved ones even though they may be far. It has the power to make my dream of democratizing knowledge a reality, of challenging my intellect, my creativity, while calling me to show restraint on how and how much I use it.

When I suggested to Sebastián and Silvina to write a book, I never thought that this idea would become a simple but comprehensive lecture on the world of the Internet without which we can no longer live. Thank you for this book, which as a good dictionary, allows me to understand and be understood, and as a good textbook, explains the reason behind every recommendation.

"

Internet excites us because it offers us the possibility of thinking globally, taking into account diversity while posing new challenges to us every day. And above all, it does so because it lets us know the results of our work through statistics and user behavior...

# ACKNOWLEDGEMENTS

Ana Rita Gonzalez: For giving us the inspiration
and the idea of writing this book.

David Moffly: For inspiring and dazzling us everyday,
analyzing statistics and "moving the online helm"
to improve performance at baeblemusic.com.

The entire team at SRP Communication & Brand
Design and SRP Interactive: For their support
on this project.

Our eternal gratitude to Ediciones B, for having first
published this book in Spanish.

Special thanks to our agents Jennie Willink and Susan
Kittenplan and the team of Will/Plan Projects for their
support and to York House Press for saying yes to
this book.

"

"Give a person a fish and you feed them for a day; teach that person to use the Internet and they won't bother you for weeks."

**Anonymous**

# ADDITIONAL CONTENT

## ✓ Checklist

A complete step by step guide to check the qualities of your Website, including the 222 Tips.

## a-z Glossary

A useful glossary that includes terms used in Web technology, so they are accessible to an owner or manager of a Website who doesn't have a technological background.

Start enjoying online material at: **www.222tips.biz**.

Smile: you are the key to your own success.

**Sebastián Pincetti** holds a B.S. degree in IT from CAECE (Center for Advanced Science Studies University) and an MBA in Management and Strategic Marketing from UCES (Business and Social Sciences University). He became a partner at SRP Communication & Brand Design in 1992 and later co-founded SRP Interactive. Previously, he ran a technology company that provided support to top of the line companies. His main responsibilities at SRP include strategic planning, development and process improvement, e-business strategies and new business development. As a member of SRP, he applies his expertise in integrating corporate image with new technologies, which allows him to enable his clients to recognize the value of a brand, one of the major assets of a company and the key to its growth. Sebastian speaks English, Spanish and Italian.

**Silvina Rodriguez Picaro** holds a B.F.A. in graphic design from the University of Buenos Aires (UBA), an M.S. in Corporate Communication Sciences from UCES (Business and Social Sciences University) and an MBA in Marketing from Universidad del Salvador and the State University of New York (SUNY). At an early age, she worked at the top design studios and advertising agencies of Buenos Aires and Sao Paulo. Her work has been recognized by numerous awards, including the Silver Pencil, highlighting her as the Designer of the Year in 1992, as the deemed by CAYC. Silvina co-founded SRP Communication Brand & Design and SRP Interactive, where she currently leads the design and communication team. Her style emphasizes contact with the client and attention to detail. Her expertise in Marketing Communications has allowed her to offer clients innovative and integrated solutions. Silvina speaks English, Spanish, French and Portuguese.

**222 Tips for doing Business on the Internet**
Version 2.0
Sebastián Pincetti • Silvina Rodriguez Picaro